A SPARROW WHO ATE THE UNIVERSE

A Hundred Pounds of Poems
in a One Pound Book

SKIP MASELLI

authorHOUSE®

AuthorHouse™
1663 Liberty Drive
Bloomington, IN 47403
www.authorhouse.com
Phone: 1 (800) 839-8640

Published by AuthorHouse 08/01/2016

ISBN: 978-1-5049-6829-4 (sc)
ISBN: 978-1-5049-6900-0 (e)

Library of Congress Control Number: 2016907989

Print information available on the last page.

Any people depicted in stock imagery provided by Thinkstock are models, and such images are being used for illustrative purposes only. Certain stock imagery © Thinkstock.

This book is printed on acid-free paper.

Because of the dynamic nature of the Internet, any web addresses or links contained in this book may have changed since publication and may no longer be valid. The views expressed in this work are solely those of the author and do not necessarily reflect the views of the publisher, and the publisher hereby disclaims any responsibility for them.

Dedicated to those beloved sojourners
with whom I've journeyed, pondered, shape-shifted,
danced, or shared deep silences.
Without your everlasting light,
I'd be invisible.

All photos/graphics by the author, unless otherwise stated.

Contents

Preface

This is a book of poetry, a lifelong, ongoing labor of love. How do I gently lead you buy the hand and heart into the depths of its contents? There, I can maybe convey each poem's transcendent meaning within you; meaning which is independent and perhaps more splendid than that which inspired me to write it.

I was eleven when I began writing poems in the margins of any piece of paper I could find. I never thought to ask for a pad of paper. Notebook computers were still a couple decades away. I remember calling *writing* my "inner out." I wrote, "Most people don't understand it, but its meaning it doth shout." Yep, I wrote in those archaic terms back then too.

In ninth grade we were asked to submit a book of poetry as a class project, after which we would be given a grade. A grade?! I wrote on the last page of my delivered poetry assignment that I thought it wrong to grade poetry because it was grading someone's feelings. Here I am, almost forty years later, publishing a book of poetry, and I have to explain within this preface why anyone should read it. And I wonder still: am I being graded? Where within the consciousness exchanged between writer and reader does a poem's quality exist?

Poetry is how some engage with the world around them. I cannot understand a world if I do not stimulate my surroundings through an understanding of myself so I might gauge its reaction. Writing is my way of poking the sleeping giant of unconsciousness. Partly from the world's reaction we learn more about about the subtlety of our life's nature and intent.

Creativity is a temptress that lives in the shadows of our being. She often reveals herself when our attentions drift away from her. So when I should be doing other things, I create. And the relationship between my writing and me has been a tumultuous one. I have fought her at every turn and fallen under her spell. I have put my writing above the immediate needs of my job, family, and partners. My writing has held me at a distance from those worldly things I love the most. So lamenting and longing becomes something sublime in my poetry. We study what is distant the most closely, and once we get too close, we create distance.

I wonder if the act of writing is itself an ode to something beyond all that I'm able to love on this earth. Am I wrong to love one thing more than everything? Perhaps we love in spirit that which exceeds the capacity of the human body. Could Pablo Neruda have been under the spell of the divine when he wrote,

> I love you without knowing how, or when, or from where.
> I love you simply, without problems or pride: I love you in
> this way because I do not know any other way of loving
> but this, in which there is no I or you, so intimate that your
> hand upon my chest is my hand, so intimate that when I
> fall asleep your eyes close.[1]

My eyes water when we cannot turn our passions away from mystery's expression; that blissful confusion - if we let it happen - when we cannot distinguish who is writer, who is reader, and what is inspiration. I'm drawn to Coleman Barks' poetic translation of a poem by the beloved Mawlana Jalāl ad-Dīn Rumi's poetry,

> All day I think about it, then at night I say it ...
>
> [b]ut who is it now in my ear who hears my voice?
> Who says words with my mouth?
> Who looks out with my eyes?
>
> This poetry, I never know what I'm going to say.
> I don't plan it.
> When I'm outside the saying of it,
> I get very quiet and rarely speak at all.[2]

I have toiled over this book's purpose before I wrote it, as I compiled it, and in hindsight. This book's completion is really the beginning of something new and so I toil over its release. Indeed, every exit is an entrance. And there are some interesting distinctions in how we understand *purpose* in the context of poetic literature and within that of writing, reading, and poetry itself.

---

[1] Pablo Neruda, 100 Love Sonnets, 1941
[2] The Essential Rumi, Translated by Coleman Barks, 2004

Poetry has no purpose,
none at all.
It seems to be
some kind of involuntary emission
from a busy mind or
a broken heart,
a clouded memory,
a longed-for future.
It has no purpose
because it does not fulfill
any of these states,
for the busy mind still toils,
the heart crumbles,
memories fail,
and the future eludes us,
remaining one word ahead
of its expression.

Poetry is a rope dropped into a coil
at the bottom of a dark pit.
Its usefulness is hardly imaginable.
Its words are square wheels on a child's go-cart
at the top of hill.
It is an untamable wild animal
being chased around by a poet
consumed by his vanity,
swinging his pen for a stick
at shadows and light.

The purpose of poetry is that
of the disembodied spirit,
cut from the palace of heaven.
And that purpose is
to seek its purpose
before it dies by the writer's mark
on the parchment of
humanity.

What is the purpose of poetry?
It is the most noble,
nonpurposeful thing
to ever dawn upon
our awareness—
no more and no less
than a wine-splashed peach sunset,

the waterfall of blue sorbet,
the velvet catkins of a pussy willow,
and the tapping
by your grandfather's ghost behind the curio cabinet or
the heart's quiver
in a lover's exhale.

Find the purpose of *these*,
and then maybe
you'll find your answer.

The function of poetry is "to please, to move, and to transport ... Poetry is the breath and finer spirit of all knowledge; it is the impassioned expression which is in the countenance of all science ... every great poet is a teacher; I wish either to be considered as a teacher or as nothing.[3]" (William Wordsworth).

My hope is for you, the reader, to draw your own lessons, find peace in your own purpose, kindle a question, and illuminate an answer, all from this book. Those who teach are teachers; those who learn become teachers. And so this book is our relationship—reader, writer, and poem.

---

[3] Lyrical Ballads, Michael Schmidt (editor), Penguin Classics, 2007

Acknowledgments

I offer my unfathomable gratitude to those amazing friends and apparitions, seen and unseen, from across the world and those placeless places that inspired, encouraged, and quite simply became the content of so much I've written. I'd especially like to thank my family—children and parents—for much more than your support, but for their love and tolerance over all those decades as I frequently drifted into aloof and reflective states.

Writing is not a talent; it's an affliction. And it can leave the author lonely, his family and friends distressed, or, on those more fortunate occasions, leaves the author surrounded with the most amazing and understanding people.

In final, I am grateful to the One and the countless steps that have been taken along life's path toward divine provenance.

Introduction

A Sparrow Who Ate the Universe: A Hundred Pounds of Poems in a One-Pound Book is an anthology of contemplations and reflections of the heart. The origin of these poems finds its way to you through a life shared deeply with and among many. They are colored in broad brush by metaphor, assonance, alliteration, and rhyme. But the true meaning of this collection is found through you, for within the soul of the beloved reader is a patient universe waiting to be written. Indeed "the poet creates anew the universe,[4]" wrote Percy Bysshe Shelley.

This anthology has four chapters, each of a different genre.

- Chapter 1 is a collection of love poems. As straightforward as it sounds, the quest both for and by human love is a fathomless topic. These poems tell stories of the following kinds of love: lost, true, divine, new, unrequited, longed-for, and love with a lowercase ("l") and uppercase ("L"). Most are catalyzed by a blend of romantic reflections, but the journey of reflective introspection traverses between the heart and mind, leading to deeper states of self-disclosure. These poems are about everyone and anything that somehow completes the archetype of "love" within the understanding of being human.

- Chapter 2 explores the mysteries of love and the love for Mystery. I first discovered the word "Khamosh" in 2013 during a period of

---

[4] David Hopkins, The Routledge Anthology of Poets on Poets, 2003

personal transformation and self-awareness, inspired by auspicious events and accompanied by the most remarkable and beloved friends and family. Like a pebble dropped through the surface of still waters, the impact of these experiences continues to ripple outward into unheard harmonies just waiting to be written and someday it will, God willing. "Who you are, what is your purpose, and what is its meaning" are questions that arc across the universe in search of answers that will finally embrace the associated longing and guide you into ecstatic completion. These poems resonate along the nexus of self and spirit and are seasoned with explorations of Sufism, philosophical studies, and other ontological jaunts taken over the past few decades. It is a spiritual read if you are a spiritualist, a religious read if you are a religionist, and a philosophical read if you are a philosopher.

- Chapter 3 is comprised of lighter, softer-sounding poems; character sketches; self-portraits of a writer (and reader); and poetic musings of the human condition that shimmers across lives and relationships. These pieces reveal deep sentiments through the unraveling of nostalgia, an intoxicant to most writers and poets. It is indeed baffling and amazing how nocturnal sounds, natural lighting at dusk, or a sucker punch to the heart sends us spiraling back through the passage of time. May these poems be kind to your heart.

- Chapter 4 includes pieces written rapidly under more austere writing conditions that reflect episodes of sarcasm, mischief, frustration, self-loathing, disgust, boredom, or playfulness—and all these from observations of the world going on around me. One might hear these poems as spoken word versus the more melodic and soft poetic diction seen elsewhere in this anthology. The language is occasionally strong, but it's not to honor the profane word. It's rather employed to illustrate the harsher nature of being among all humankind and how we cannot always tune our filters to sift out the chaff without losing some of the nutrition of the wheat.

You may find inspiration and disagreement here. They may leave you curious or informed. Whatever the case, spring forth from these as a writer, an opponent, a comrade, and a lover of the divine. As the writer, I only own the words. You own the meaning.

This book's title, *A Sparrow Who Ate the Universe*, comes partly from a poem contained within this book, not one of particular notoriety, mind you, but I always found it interesting. While eating al fresco one day in New York City, I was observing a sparrow hopping inquisitively around a large loaf of bread left on top of a recently vacated restaurant table. The loaf was so heavy. There was no way even a larger seagull or raven could carry it off.

The bird was all alone with this huge feast to herself. But then she jumped out from her orbit around the boule and landed on the ground below the table. She began nibbling up the crumbs fallen from the loaf. I sensed this immense joy in this tiny animal's movements. And I thought, with so much bread on top of the table, the real fulfillment for the sparrow comes from the remaining tiny crumbs on the ground beneath it, with which it now fills its belly to its limits and beyond the limitless capacity of the spirit.

The universe responds to the capacity of our need from its unfathomable bounty and not beyond that. The sparrow is not drawn to the amount of bread that fills the universe; rather she seeks to fill her soul on the simplicity of "bread-ness" there among the attributes of the cosmos. Whether a few crumbs or the entire loaf, bread is bread.

Let's break bread together. Bon appetit, dear reader!

Skip Maselli
April, 2016

Chapter 1

There Is a Pearl Within You

Introduction

It is always about love, isn't it? I chose the title of this chapter from the following *poemette* appearing in my first book, *Twenty-Five Words toward the Truth—#25wtT*.

There are pearls in you
So I'll slip without splash
Into the pools between your lashes
For the eyes have depths
Only lovers can dive.

I'm sometimes asked if there is someone in particular I'm writing about in these poems. More often than not, the answer is no. Of course a blend of romantic reflections catalyze them, but the journey of reflection traverses between the heart and mind. The direction of that journey leads to deeper states of my own self-disclosure, and I end up writing about no one particular, but rather everyone and everything that somehow completes the archetype of love within the understanding of my being. Yes, there are particular people among the totality - but where does one focus? I'm reminded of a saying quoted by so many in so many places, "Where do I flee from your presence? Thou art everywhere."

This collection is not intended as rhyming, rhythmic lessons or simple dictums for lovers. Many are belletristic rather than quintessential deep dives into the mystical truths of love—although some do attempt to traverse along the nexus of divine love and human love, with an emphasis on "human." Within this book is another chapter of poems called "Whispers of a Silent Heart (Khamosh Dil ki Sarghoshiyan[5])," which does explore the deeper questions and mysteries of divine and exquisite love.

Encouraged by friends, I attempt to narrate the meanings of some of these poems at their ends, but then I just end up writing another poem. You see, the reading of anything poetic sparks a wildfire in the heart, at least for those inclined to burn. I hope fire rages within all those who read this book so they might be inspired to go out and kindle the world.

These poems are not organized by any inherent characteristic or sequence with respect to their meanings. Feel free to skip around in your reading. I do make some attempt to mix long and short poems, as it can be tiresome to read them in strict order.

You will also see that I've taken great liberty with punctuation, wordplay, structure, mixed meter, along with alliteration, assonance, and consonance. This is how love goes. It takes liberties and finds its own harmony in disarray and cacophony. Love does everything it can to romance the edges right off the jagged rules.

Please let yourself fall into your own being as you read them. I hope you never back love into a corner in your endless pursuits, but I do hope it surrounds you.

---

[5] Translation from Urdu

The Waiting Rings of Time

Waiting in my memory,
Its gentle waves are calling me,
For I too was cut from eroding shore
To ocean's edge forevermore.

Never a sight had crossed my eyes,
So vast a nexus, land and sky,
And sea. Transfixed, so there I stood
In briny sand by drifting wood,

While still, each visage yet untamed,
Each weathered bough, not one the same.
To touch them all, I sought to soothe
With salted kisses, lay them smooth.

There among the writhing forms,
I walked barefoot and weather worn.
While each piece begged my presence to stay,
Another hurried me on my way.

What could quench this thirsting gaze?
Lo, is all for destination's sake?
I beg for but a moment longer,
With all these twisting paths to ponder.

I too am driftwood on the beach,
A wilting flower within your reach.
One day You'll have me by Your side
and unbury my waiting rings of time.

Breakfast with a Writer

Softly I'll land
wherever you alight
and slide over the lee of your wake.
I'll drift on your breath
and fly on stirred winds
to wherever your wings will take.

I'll break my fast
with steel-cut oats,
sip the steam of splendid tea,
and dip my bread
in the yolk of love.
And you'll adore the dawn
with me.

Sated Reflections

Let's not run from reflections,
Whether they be of you or me,
Whether by light or mirror glow,
By whom it's shown or who it shows,
Be it my darkness or flattery.

To recite what is in one's true heart
Is the sound of a rose opening.
The reddening stealth of its petals felt,
Opening for rainwater's gathering.

From one's lips, another sips
The other's poem, a cup,
Into which to pour the other's evermore.
Can another's other ever fill enough?

And should that rose be clipped or closed,
Tilt its flower, and fall to earth,
Is nothing wasted in reflections tasted?
By bud to bloom, all love is birth.

Beauty makes the heart lose balance,
Spinning circles in the foam of the mind.
'Tis not important which turn is last,
Be it hoops of hope or rings of past.
All soulful gaze, through unknown waves,
Is forever remembered as a fragrance cast.

Parindey

Only a wind whines
here in my heart,
where ghosts once sojourned.
They've all departed
since you arrived,
since you stepped through.

These eyes are doors
to wider shores,
so green, once blue,
now as brown as yours.

Sometimes a stranger's light arrives
to show itself or you, despite
your tear-choked stealth,
that fruitless tries
to run, resist, be still, and hide.

So fell a feather from the sky
from the wing of a beloved passerby.
So many hues within this plume,
I thought it leapt off reposeful perch,
from the cradle of a crescent moon.

A while longer may you stay,
O lovely, pining *parindey*.
But if you must return to sea,
then send more feathers for my wings,
and I'll join you when you fly away.

***

Parindey is an Urdu word for "bird." But I think it's more about the nature of the bird, whose beauty compels so many to contain it (clip its wings) that we take away its "bird-ness." *Parindey* cannot help but fly. It is beyond the bird; it is flight disembodied from the feather.

Smithereens

Love's mystery unraveling
is a star burning out,
naught but a flame without its coal,
a constellation sans axis
to circle about.

When its meaning exceeds
the object of dreams,
let it go.
Let it go to be loved
to smithereens.

***

Out of habit, many fathom love in purely mental constructs, fitting it within a time-space context. They desperately try to put terms to it. Some can sadly only identify with it through its object. This poem is about loving beyond subject and object.

Sisters of Darkness

Her eyes are the sisters of darkness
who, upon their hearts, glisten
as starry amulets of the night.

She speaks not,
but listens for his words
and waits for sparks to ignite.

One wish is for what we lack;
the other is a prayer
for what we deserve.

If he grants her wish
but ignores her prayer,
of what use does this love serve?

***

There is confusion between "falling in love" and "being in love."

The Pearl of Wisdom

To look into the eyes of she who sees me
is a supplication to a light I emit,
and within her is an echo and glowing ember.
I too become the billows of destiny's sender,
and my beloved's torch is lit.

As a poet, I saw the world with my heart.
As a lover, I stirred open the eyes of Shiva to Shakti.
As a seeker, I took the pearl of wisdom from her lips with mine.
As a man, into the mystic abode of love, I was set free.

We pause in pinwheel reflections of all this
to catch the translucent patterns in the veil
and, with gentle hands, wave away the mist,
as the winds of once wishes begin to fulfill our boat's waiting sails.

We sojourn not to find our fortune's ends
in the gazes and embraces of lovers or friends.
Rather we come to find ourselves in the other,
and there, we find our fortune begins.

***

The eyes of the lover hold the expressive reflection of what we emit. They respond to the intentions of our hearts. Like blackbodies, they radiate back all they absorb.

Morning of the Madrugada

While I press my palm to hers,
I want to complete the world
as our fingers fold into the fabric of the skin.

I ache to taste the tongue of my lover,
to wash away the flavor of mango
so I'll never seek a sweeter fruit again.

As I close my eyes in the blackening,
I want to hear her, raining
star drops into my night.

I imagine my last jar of breath, taken,
its lid twisted off and emptied into providence.
Then she fills the slack sails within me.

All I need for my humility
is to be placed gently
in the vessel of her beauty

and then pushed softly from the dunes
into a stock-still ocean, sans a single ripple,
saffron petals, long leaves, and a softening moon.

Oh, to love her in unrepeatable ways
and never miss a moment
of us ever having done so.

Her pulse is the only sound imagined
when nightingales go silent,
when winds' wisps are somnolent.

From the mystery of my heart as I sleep,
my muse glides through the darkness,
into the morning of the *madrugada*.

Wild Vine

We are each alone
and together everywhere.
Not a molecule of you do I contain.
Refresh your beauty where you need,
for you travel like a wild vine
in search of falling light.
But your roots run deep into me,
Oh beloved, I will bring you the earth,
and you will bring me beyond.

***

Not even the greatest love is meant to be. There is a time and place, and we must adhere to this. We have no choice. The buried seed of love contains a universe—root, nourishment, and the vines that reach above the soil and head toward the skies. One of you might be the roots from that seed, holding fast to the earth; the other might be the wild growing vine from the very same seed of love. There's nothing you can do. Just let go. Be.

Another Morning Awoken by Night

I hear a first whistle of a bird
just before the dance of dawn.
And dew drips down
the cat-tongued blades of
a softening, sprawling lawn.

A humming bread truck in the distance
makes its way toward a loading dock
behind a humble store bakery
with a donut for a wall clock.

Tangent to the arc of a hesitant sun rising,
the air begins to eddy,
swirling through the porch door screen,
hissing, java ready, steady.

There's a subtlety in the rising chorus
of kisses between the new spring leaves,
waking the budding flowered branches
whispering harmoniously on the breeze.

Turning dreams stroke the linen,
white and twisted all about
and through it.
Our skin slightly shivers within.
By this morning we are bound.

You stir gently to again drift off,
and I am so in love.
This suburban morning aviary
hears the persistent cooing of a dove.

Sunlight ripens from cerulean to rouge
and curls its streams all over you.
The morning murmurs sleepily
as a new day rinses off the dew.

Another morning's awoken by night,
shepherding our hearts to slumber,
this eternal reprise of celestial cycles.
Love arrives to allay the night
in dawn's awaiting wonder.

I Dreamt You Wrote a Poem

I dreamt you wrote a poem,
and I read it in my sleep.
I woke in low light to find it true.
It shone my eyes, every word of you.

My arms too have become my wings.
You do this to me;
I do this to you.
We are twinning spirals helix,
birds in flight, we two.

Once a heart is unlocked from its belief
that it was ever in a cage,
it sees the cage as a door-less home
and forever flies away.
It soars in dreams by night
and returns to perch by day.

Pulsing Inkwell

Love's letters clatter in currents.
Winds curl to stillness
in a talus of potpourri.

Season totem,
a cluster of hope,
waiting for one match pulled and struck
to scare the ghosts
from the pyre
in a choke of smoke from sweet attar.

Love's heat
fans the embers within
the heart's own fire.

So many words
wrenched from mouth
and wrought from hand
contortions,
a twisted spoken grip.

We strip the evergreen needles
from the bough
and let them fall from the fist,
sprinkling fir
to the earth as grist.

Had not a sentence stretched from
the pulsing inkwell
by plume to parchment or
from warm breath of lip's beseech,
what then of our night would say
and of our day to listen?

If we do not dare with deeds to fly,
then the falling never ends.
And poem eternal ne'er to begin
loves expression, not its desire.
It is the cachet
to which both life and death aspire.

***

    Love is a thing of action. Falling in love eventually becomes "just love."
And just love is exalting. It's like flying.

Birds of a Song

Rain paths brush clear a sky
to stark, beautiful disclosure.
I listen to her notes of doubt,
softly singing through the azure.

With dove's ear low, I listen on
for another who perchance is
a muse, perched atop a pendulous pen,
swaying lithely among the branches.

Music is written of moments when
she trusts my song.
Its combs of rain
are sheared in harmony from soaring wing
from I,
the melodious bird himself,
who's ever to fly away again.

Sibilant Skin

When still,
the world turns around the axis of my heart.
From the dark within,
lemniscates of a lantern light
tie ribbons in my eyes.
Will you know me then?

And when I die,
a steady, sibilant wind
of myrrh and frankincense
will polish my bones,
so that when you see me again,
I'll glow anew
through a translucent veil
of sweetly scented skin.

***

Lovers lost to each other in life die to find each other in the after-ness, to walk together in the garden of Imran.

Everything

Everything we see is
its pristine essence
casting the same light
from the womb of darkness.

Gripped by the dolor of a glaucous sky,
love's longing reminds us
that nothing is ever truly lost
to anything less
than the visual acuity of a heart.

Unseen signs never give up
their quest for being seen.
With a slight tilt of the head,
the light of the heart changes,
and so does everything ...
everything.

***

Love is never lost, just its object. It's a matter of how we choose to look at our fate. The heart continues to see love long after its object has expired. It is the purest form of love. Everything can be a sign. The world is filled with them, and the senses are relentless in their pursuit to pass to the mind any reminder it might be seeking. Indeed, if you just look at the word differently, the light from your emanating heart actually changes, casting light on everything. Your heart becomes the sign maker.

Poems That Will Get Me Killed

I wrote to her sacrilege,
toasting our haram.
She is an idol among dregs;
I am a totem in her palm.

Love lifts on a rose scent,
leaving petals to quiver
all between us once, rent,
with only kindling to give her.

Hence, I turn to death,
which best knows life,
and set fire to my nest
for guiding torchlight
to illuminate the path
on my way home
to weep love.
Ere I die
for writing this poem.

Message to the Beloved Reader before I'm Killed

Go down dark and deep beloveds
it's good to go to those dark places within,
it's there that we burn
and into that fire,
we dip our unlit torches
to light our way out again.
go blind in your own light
and descend,
for many a stirred soul
will sway and rustle
in the same divine wind;
and all this
to fill the spirit's silent wing
by which your voice ascends.

***

Love poems can be where the lost lover becomes the discovered love. This poem builds upon the idolatrous, possessive love that sometimes grips us harder than we grip that which we love. We kill ourselves in the process of killing the real beauty of that which we love. Love has its own standards for heresy. Be true to the truth of love. You know what it is. Strip away the idols, the fair skin, and dark sinuous hair and chiseled physique. If you don't see it, you're not in love. And sadly it might be the right person; you're just unable to see him or her. You're in darkness, and who knows what will find you in there.

The Romance of Muse and Artist

She is a tress of hair out of place,
combed in slow sweeps from my forehead.
I thought of her as an enigma to perchance unravel
by the press of well-paired lips
or a mind besotted with moon glow
and Grenache wine,
one wicked seduction by wisdom's kiss,
saccharine words stirred into woody coffee.

I, Whitman, imagine her
as the chill of Robert Frost,
clung like sugar grains to my *Leaves of Grass*.
Almandine eyes of the nine Mousai
revved up by unbridled inventiveness.

I twinge too much to hold it inside;
she triumphs beyond the rim of her vessel,
so our ache and exultation
steal past the musing sentinel of apprehension
and leap from once-dormant imagination
into splendid motifs of spirit shadows.

She is a stranger to all
but to those whom she whispers as *lover*.
We, two strangers of sun and moon,
curl nubile into night
to take our nuptials at dawn.

One hundred million miles and
one earth between us;
now bound as one, we pull the tides
into an unexpected tempest in my heart,
a tender act of indiscretion
undoing a tame, near tepid bearing.

Thus muse and artist
feast upon the provender of providence
and all delectable in between them.

My Magnificent Morning Malaise

I pour the wine while you raise your cup
until our bodies have had enough
that our spirit's twist, wrung out dry,
sexed and sated.
Shyly truth seeps outside
of careless vessels,
free once more,
unable to collide,
despite this ardor.

Our thoughts clashed clandestine,
while our demeanors remain docile.
Your scowl is the bone beneath a smile;
our rose skin kisses, turning hostile.
There is the quaff of a tongue,
the taunting touch.
Skin chenille beneath blankets blush.

Suddenly sensitive to the sounds of dawn,
a trash truck groans,
and someone mows a lawn.
Last night's dream bent around a *now* that's gone.
Time has stopped, but it still goes on and on.

I'm up;
you're naked.
Every morning maunders, overmedicated.
Every house is a story;
every window is perspective.
My window is dark;
theirs is a beverage
to fill a voyeur's empty cup with scornful slake,
set to brew when strangers wake,
having gone to bed not knowing each other,
in the morning, they wake as broken lovers.

***

Skip Maselli

We go through this dementia when we reminisce about a beautiful lost lover. It's a tad jaded, but it's mostly intended to honor the sensuality of lovers. Even the ending is exotic and sensual. I somewhat contrast it at the end, leaving the reader to imagine the contrast of having the same exact sex with two different people, but it's just real with one and not the other. It's a fine line between a lover and real love.

Earthbound Elements in Repose

Of earthbound lovers in repose,
darkness awakens dreams for those
who, in their arrogance, sleep so well
with their sinuous curves that writhe in hell.

Fleeting words leap to a tragic death
off the end of a sentence's precipice,
spoken by guardians of empty spaces
whose wings are clipped by periphrasis,
writing ghazals that shadows recite
to ghosts who gather to find respite.

Yet these mortal instruments of a soul's confession
are sung to the Beloved for intercession.
Still enlightened fools in darkness will part
with the keys to unlock another's heart.

Spires of ice from obsidian skies
land and melt in the warmth of their eyes,
drowning their captains in waves of emotion,
so two continents drift and collide in the ocean.

'Tis Her Again

She is a crazy thing
Who walks on air
With her limber ways
And mussed-up hair.

So the sooner I find her,
By heart or by head,
I care little which one
So long there's a bed.

'Tis the bottle that waits
For her lips to taste
Its content within.

'Tis her again
Who drinks of the wine
To skirt distance and time.

So when love comes to hold her,
'Tis the bottle that's sober.

I'm sorry I wrote
These horrible poems.
It would not be the case
If she only came home.
I'd have nothing say.

Love's Fool and Fortunate One

He was love's fool,
a drop of rain,
in a downpour of seasonal shame.
A farthing in the fountain
spent on wishes,
glistening in the fenlands
of unreplenished riches.
A plea among the rustling
in a vast forest of variegated leaves.
Sorrow among garrulous winds
gusting.

A path through
his wooded pathos
blazed with love and lusting.
When a tear finds wing
on a falling leaf
snapped from the limbs
by currents of heat
rockabye'd into halcyon.
So misery and his aerie companion
forge a new coin
in an empty hand that is
thrown and flipping along an arc.

A pinwheel casting solar sparks,
purls hope in a tumbling fall
that promises anything can happen
to anyone,
anytime
at all.

***

You and your lover might find each other before the wish. Then forge
the coin that one of you throws into the fountain, wishing for what you
already have. This is a self-portrait of sorts. I have such high ideals of love.
The coin is forged and thrown. I just need to be ready to receive the wish.

We Lie at Night

I dream.
She lies
with her eyes open.
Flying fish leap
between two placid oceans,
catching moonlight
on their silver scales.

I wake.
She lies awake,
not seeing
that I watch her
talk to God.

I can tell from her fathomless gaze,
and I am amazed
at how far her eyes
can see.

She lies;
I lie woken in each other's eyes,
my pond and her ocean.
I drift in her devotion
to seek beyond measure,
yet it's not the conquest
of her vision,
but of the silence
in her surrender.

She lies awake,
dreaming.
My eyes opened,
sleeping.

At sea, it's
us three:
me, an angler of stars,
the Beloved,
and thee.

***

This is a Sufi love poem mixed with a bit of human love and the modern dilemma as lovers try to figure out how much and in what ways they love, and often this is a futile or disappointing activity. In the struggle, there's wrong decisions and delusions. The word "lie" is meant to be ambiguous. It could me being prostrate or not telling the truth (but not maliciously lying, almost like lying to oneself about another).

Hibiscus Dreams

She throws words underhand with her mouth.
The boy leans in past natural borders
to study the agenda in her eyes.
He is built like a bent paperclip
with bottlebrush forelocks and a barracuda jaw.

Between her bare legs, she gently squeezes
a cup of iced hibiscus tea.
She reaches down and lifts it to her lips.
I feel mine part in thirsting sympathy.

Her upper thighs blush wet with condensation as
the boy's eager fingers click on her knee.
Like ice cubes in her sweating berry hibiscus,
floral melt cascades down her throat.

Fairy breath lands on my shoulders,
my silk overcoat.
It makes me dissolve with memory
of my beloved tea picker,
a cocoa-skinned Sudanese girl
traveling the road to market in Al-Junaynah,
swaying in the truck bed under a warm sun,
dreaming of red karkadeh flowers
and a paperclip boy.

***

This is a sensual poem with double entendre. I was somewhat thinking of Steinbeck's book, *Grapes of Wrath*, with the descriptions of two men fixing a car, whose components are feminized so the passage seems to describe sex with a woman. This dear Sudanese girl is real, and there is something mysterious and elusive about her to the boy, who clearly is enamored with her. He's probably not particularly good-looking. But she likes that he likes her, and we feel this odd sort of love between them that perhaps goes beyond romance and heads into the comforts of aesthetic familiarity.

Unseen Heart

"You are sacred to Me,"
speaks a steep, disembodied voice
lifted by the lowly,
rescued by the reed,
quenched by the eagle.

She has been delivered to the underworld
from sliding scree,
heading into silence
from the long sigh of a still black flag
hung for her Eros.

The one was raised by no one,
pounded into poet,
scorched by doubt,
and blessed with scars.

The doubting beloved is dancing,
despairing,
the impossible possible.

Her solemn spin stirs open the rose petals
far away in a waiting redolent garden
that is thirsting a tear from Proserpina,
weeping for the company of a nightingale.
The Beloved arrives with blood-red wine.

"You are the sacred of the sacred
for Your heart has eyes and
I've no wings of fire, nor beast I be.
See my unseen heart
and I'll return to Thee."

***

This is about another poem which will be revealed in some other book, some other time. There is a beauty to what remains unseen. It is a sanctum in which unspoken words echo off the walls in an ever-deepening silence.

To Die for Love

The illusion of love for another
is a manifestation of a secret
withheld from us by God.

As such,
those we love cannot darken our lives,
for what illuminates them
is a reflection of a Truth
beyond death.

Those that carry the candle for you,
may not have lit the flame.

***

True love is recalled, not made. And once it arrives, we find it came from within us and will not be compared to anything or anyone. Two people can release one fragrance of love. Once released though, neither can return it to the bottle. They may go their separate ways by death or dead, but the scent pleasantly follows, but not as a reminder of the other. Instead it's of the fathomless love we already have within us. The inner source illuminates love for others, it is divine. The persistence of love cannot be refused; it is not ours to deny, it is not simply given, it is endowed.

Surrounded by Ourselves

Those whom we surround with hatred
surround us,
and so it goes with love.

Love surrounds those
who surround others with love.
The struggle begins and ends
with how you circumscribe yourself.

Hatred is fear tied to a soul.
Love is letting go of the rope.
We are weary of strife
and long for love.

To be moved in even the slightest way
by words of love
is an ember of hope in a darkened hearth,
waiting for a breeze
to raze the flame again.

Stillness in the Balance

Our broken hearts beat loudly,
pounding away at the diamond-hard surface of love
with soft, golden hammers,
looking for a whole to perhaps
take a chip out of
or find more gold with which to make more hammers
to replace those that have become blunt.

The irony is that the love we seek
we wield in our very own hands,
and the truth is that love cannot be broken in two,
no matter how much it bends.

I have three loud clocks in this room,
each set for a different longitude on earth.
One ticks for the future somewhere west;
the other tocks for the past toward the east.
In between is the one rhythm I wish to hear most,
that which counts the moment of the here and now.

The love we treasure is not buried in the past
or waiting in the future.
Find the restless hearts such as ours.
Love like another,
and we will love no other.

These lost moments are the underpinnings
of a forever that is behind us.
Pause tenderly in this moment,
and you may indeed find that love stands due before you.

The paradox is
that we all share in the labors of love and strife,
too busy to find the stillness in their balance.

Byzantine Kiss

Her whispers writhe upward, warming my lips,
chased gently by thoughts and fingertips

that pulse over keys, sewing words onto fields
of love's thirsty parchment, tenderly peeled

from shavings off banyan trees, twisted in time,
woven from tangles of roots and vines

that glimmer and glide on the twirls of her hair
that coil around dreams as they swirl in the air

and reciprocate whispers that blend into sighs,
reflecting like moonlight in opening eyes.

Honey-silk visage and java, like brindle,
eyes like flint against frizzen will kindle.

Fire in the heart calls men once missing
to a resplendent nexus of lost souls kissing.

Arcadian journeys of body and mind
sing from fathomless depths of space and time.

Geography traversed by her steps, sublime,
bearing *piedra de ijada* from a Far Eastern mine.

Electricity leaps in passionate arcs,
from skin to skin in dendritic sparks

that strobe over rhythm beneath the sheets,
as lovers listen and friction speaks

in syncopation with shuddering breaths
from sodden mouths that sweetly press.

And I close my eyes in synchronicity,
but even closed, it's her I see,

tasting the salt of a single tear,
a harbinger for the moments near.

High on the hum, hopes embrace
as rapture and destiny hasten the pace.

I open my eyes to watch her go,
but once inside it starts to grow

into a poem unleashed in my heart
by a byzantine kiss after lost lips part.

Driftwood in Your Ocean

When I am silent,
I am down in my imagination.

I am swimming
across the surface of your eyes,
seeing the sea beneath them.
Their currents are upwelling,
such a sweet and quiet place,
your eyes.

I am driftwood in your ocean.
You flow above and below.

Never mistake my silence for absence.
I seek your presence in the pause,
where the seed of a poem prepares.

I've fallen asleep to the essence of you
many evenings,
searching for what you
already hold
and offer
in a kiss.

***

These are excerpts from things I'd written, assembled by a beloved friend into a poem. So this is really a collaboration of sorts; so *mahalo* for seeing the diamond in the rough!

Rose Petals Falling in the Garden

Memories fade to susurrus.
Dusk casts shadows rising o'er the temple wall.
Amber skin,
maternal fields,
upon soft abdomen,
his ear falls.

Below the peel of empyrean
is the fruit of a woman,
Brave is the man who clings to the rind,
but braver is he who lets go in time.

Saccharine,
she whose taste is closest
to touch the Beloved's face.
Pressed, he hears her oceans howl,
hurling hope upon the waves.

To love a woman thus
is to be born to her
and then to die
over and over again.
Upon his brow, lips land.
Her winter eyelids close,
falling and falling in the garden.
Go the petals of the rose.

***

There's an eternal love, though lovers may part. This is a poem on this bittersweet essence.

The Passenger

Was it frightening when I went away?
I miss you when I used to know you.

"I suppose. Were your journeys difficult?
Because I'm still here, climbing, and I miss you too."

I would often scan the signaling stars
and wish you'd have just come with me instead.

"I would have, but I was swallowed by silence
in the shadows of the wooded edge."

And I was entranced with the hues on the horizon,
wishing only to slip away with the seagoing fleet.

"And I could feel the mountain breeze at my back
and the sweet scent of seasons shifting below my feet."

I watched as you turned toward the trail.

"While I saw you step into the whispering surf."

Sad and confused, I felt my heart deflate.

"Aye, so heavy, I thought mine would burst."

Then came a voice within a voice.

As the passenger, I watched each of you,
traveling the course of creation.
I delivered your lessons along the other's path
and, through each other, revealing your station.

Hope waits hidden beyond the reaches,
free from the hands of time.
You have nothing without your faith in the other,
and yet all you have is Mine.

Every deep sea and soaring mountain
returns us to unite along destiny's coast,
so never abandon your own truth's calling.
For in the end, where you began falling,
is a passenger's heart that awaits you both.

Fashioner of Wind

Layla is the faint attar at dawn,
quiet, sinuously flowing,
slowly in the morning.
She stirs the fashioner of winds.

Majnun is the feather.
Whenever his beloved gets too close,
upon her wings,
he flies off and away again.
As if the wind and quill were one.

And Finally We Sleep

Heartbeat, let me breathe good-bye,
a shooting star in her midnight sky.
Just one more breath for a candle flame
to slip the grasp of a love in vain.
Night-curled bodies, pressed and warm,
rose petal kisses to quell the storm.

We both knew, but still we held
each other tightly, breaking spells
cast by those who came before
and left behind an open door.
Now I'm lost on this path you chose.
So as I go, you'll hear it close.

I'm not who I was with this hurt inside,
but I am who I am, and I never lied.
The painful carving of deliberate words,
your eyes could be such pretty swords
to catch their flash in a glimpse of time
when I told myself that you were mine.

I held you close, and close you dreamed
of things so far away it seemed.
I close my eyes, my ears, my heart.
Release your hand, and then depart.
Wake up, Dulcinea, wherever you are.
Find your way home before you dream too far.

The Kiss that Toppled the World

Out in the surly seas,
a tidal wave toppled out of the sky,
conjured by the secret teamwork of moon and sun
from a once-gentle ripple,
and that stirred by a wondering kiss
that broke the benign surface of time. White.

There in the perpetual midnight,
souls surface and submerge
in the violent wake of love
that lays out its victims
and then lifts them up,
drowning and reviving them all at once. Black.

Like a deep red rose petal
gliding softly along a shining silk sheet,
rippling sinuously
in concert with an ocean breeze,
careening through sheer blinds
in an unfastened window. Blue.

Waves lunge and finally collapse
and roll up the thirsting sand, gleaming.
And the two, sand and water, slide back to sea

in a chorus of never-ending crashing wave on wave,
the exhalation of sea foam and muffled chimes
of churning shards of broken shells. Yellow.

Other than sunlight and ocean air
softening edges in the seaside room,
it is empty and thick with anticipation
for my companion until you come back.
For now, footprints on the beach
only pass by. Colorless.

***

There is truly a beautiful and tragic story behind this, a kiss in a rural town between two people who took on the world with the odds against them. They fell in love, and their lives fell apart (but to be reborn again). This is a long, desperate, and horribly sad story, but it is a testament to the power of love. It can topple worlds. How do the colors make you feel?

The Phoenix

I remember being so madly in love.
I look into the images of the past and realize
that we can never go back.
Loving someone so deeply dislodges and slips away
into heaven by the divine inhale.

We turn love from copper
to fiery blinding gold,
and then it is to be returned.

Love is God's alchemy, a consuming fire
delivered to lovers in the illuminated mist of God's breath.
And from this,
we are rendered to ashes that
dissipate into the breezes of remembrance.

In my years, what's left of me eddies in the dust devils
that dance at dusk.
I admire the pressed lips of sea and land
on these soft, swelled sand dunes,
envious of their kiss,
which hers and mine once rivaled.

Our days are one of precious memories and
bits of drama in the making,
sewn seeds of tenderness.
There is a self-disclosure here that,
once we love the human out of each other,
what remains is pure spirit.
We become bone-dry and quenched all the same.

Oh, lament, the sun settles
from golden gaiety to smoke gray.
And all creatures seen dormant repose.

Then in a gesture of compassion,
curious with the darkness,
morning slowly peeks over the horizon
with its thin arc of clarity.
So stirs the dawn.

The quest is to blow gently into the ashes,
to see what ember within you still glows.
Therein lies your phoenix,
your firebird.
Look into your own ruins
for your true love.

I Like Everything About This

I like how the barista knows my name and drink by heart.
I like the way the cold air licks my earlobes
and the serpentine patterns of white sand
scurrying across the black pavement.
I like the way a monkey's gaze
reminds me of my grandfather's pensive eyes.
I like those too.
I like the way your eyes purse kisses
when they delight in small poems
written on the underside of high clouds.
I like everything about this.

The Road

Do not love a love so readily given.
Let it love you and abrade,
to sink lightly to its caress.
Love is not the road you're on.
Rather you are the road,
under its steps.

I am a bridge you cross
over dark water's mystery
and jagged things that cut your flesh.
Of cobbles and trusses
built of eyes and arms, mine,
you walk tenderly through my chest.

We are the road we're on,
journeying in all directions.
We let go, we topple, and we overfill,
surrendering to whims and wills.
The pavement varnish sets and shines
from the blood we lovers spill.

We Loved Once When We Were Young

Warrior hearts leap from drunken ships,
listing in the grizzly brine.
Waves with claws to rip the prey
feast and vomit on a thin shoreline.

Swells roll in the wake of Neptune,
singing a lullaby, rippling the cloth
of angels, still and watching,
frozen by the sea in the froth.

Cadence in shadows in a choke green forest
chased hard over pine needles and moss.
My lover is close and bellicose
as I dash toward the pale, pitted docks.

Fate, the fickle savior, longs to be free,
to converge and diverge like braided streams of time,
dancing, hearts leaping, touching, and fleeing,
in the long shadows of dusk sublime.

There I am,
mesmerized by silent play between two little girls,
taking turns at each other's braids.
Cupped by soft fronds beneath the curve of a palm,
their calm was in concordance and apposition.
Their luminous jewels are not hidden by lids and lashes,
rather through reticence,
I'd catch sun glinting off the pools in their eyes,
like little honey-dipped pearls.
How they would preen and twirl each tress,
braids of time in a slow dance.

We walked with palms pressed
through pinwheels of light and long shadows,
stillness all around
except for the slow drop of the sun behind the trees,
telling life stories in a symphony of words
that welled up from our hearts to our mouths,
hovering over our silhouettes,
like musical notes
orbiting the locks of cherubim and seraphim,
preening and twirling out strands of curls,
fueling the light in our eyes,
which are forever warm fires
calling the other home.

Fractured Light

Even shadows choose to whirl
lithely in the beams,
romancing other silhouettes,
seeking revelation in their dreams.

Compassion, do not hasten them.
Nor wake them from repose.
For in the moment two dreams alight,
the awoken lover glows.

Stand boldly in love's mystery
as slings and arrows sail.
Through the strident journey, hush.
Listen for the nightingale,
whose song seeps through a cloven heart,
mending fragments into one.
Seek the source that hides unbroken
in the brilliance of the Beloved's sun.

Autumn Left a Note

She mounted the breeze
that shook the trees,
bringing our love to its knees.

"I'm not jaded.
Please look at me,
look deeply, and say good-bye."

She rustles the rust from the waving limbs.
"Here's your beloved azurite sky."
It's raining saffron and crimson leaves.

As Autumn throws on her coat,
she's gone again,
and all I have
are the tears she left on this note.

Resonance and Reticence of Words

Subsonic and thick,
poetic, obstinate words
pedal their legs in the air
like wild, restive horses
thrash and writhe
in dry, rotted halters.

Dismounted riders with edgy
eyes flashing from shadowy corners of stalls,
hold fast to your leads.
And I'll stay fast on the keys
as I sit here with heat in my lap.
A tongue swells and arches,
bathed in Montepulciano.
Words, wine, and spittle
dry sweetly on my lips.
It will not be a poem tonight,
but a kiss that speaks my rhymes and meter.

With no other pair to press,
love rears up on its haunches,
and I lick my lips anxiously.
It is the soft taste of peace and calm,
lingering in the pause.

Words push open the gates
and walk out onto the World Wide Web.

Poetry Is a Mistress

The subtlety of my sultriness
cannot hide in the tempest of her eyes.
We catch each other's meter
across the crowded parlor
and steal off to the wings
for sodden romantic whispers.

Her muted presence is a cloud born
particle of dust,
gathering the purest droplets
to fall and
falling waters accrete
into mighty earth-churning rivers.

Shamefully, perhaps by nature of a poet,
my proclivity is to paint nuances up
like a dime-store tart
and parade her around in metaphors
under my propped writing arm.
Oh, how these nuances matter.

Worthy to Love

When you know yourself—
I mean truly know the bone and sinew
holding you upright in the mirror
from felted creases along folded chits of memory
to the dog-eared pages of emotional reminder—
when your margins are filled with faded scribbling,
and when you know what ails you
and you stop selling it as fodder for attention,
then you learn to be loved.

Prodigal lovers sweep in like gales,
fraying the tips of each other's sails.
These careless wave runners of contraband
capsize and drown as a woman and man.
Love travels deep in the hulls of a human,
yet we are unseaworthy vessels
for such precious cargo.

Tend to the cracks in the architecture
of bridges that it starts to stir.
Be the splash when the glaciers calve
and plummet into the surf.
Moan with self-awareness.
Crumple into mass.
Fold and melt into flowing glass.
Tie into braids of confluent streams.
And cool into crystals of adamantine.

Love me like you're the lost puzzle piece in my identity.
What we are unable to discover within ourselves,
we find in the love of another.

Turning Out the Beasts

These beasts of burden are stubborn,
like my heart is resolved at times,
but so beautiful to watch.
Power is suspended in the tender grace
of whatever wild things dream.

And you've flung open the gates of wonderment,
and I'm casting prose like wildflower seeds
into soulful winds.
And they fly like confetti foil
into the sky and disappear to the west.

So when you next see blinking stars
on a field of cobalt blue
or scintillation on the surface of a stream,
know that it's my poem,
chased to the furthest corners of your mind
by the whip-snap sound of my pen in a storm.

I'm just resting on the high fences,
watching my words grazing in the solace of your heart,
which catches tears from the almandine eyes
of beasts that run silent through the pastures.

Sweetly as One

'Tis my turn tonight to lower the moon.
By morning you'll raise the sun.
We each reach out, oceans apart,
across distances, sweetly as one.

Carried along the waves of color,
swaying lithely in aurora's light,
we dance in cadence to symphonies
beyond stars we spin from sight.

Cresting seas and zephyrs below us
overtake the silent procession of time.
The universe pauses to the beat of your heart
bound in the echoing chambers of mine.

Ascending the inhale of heavenward breath
aloft in the dust of silver moonbeams,
two souls collide among those who arrived
to find union through the braided journey.

Cast from the sigh of mystery,
through others' lives we spun,
two lost lovers return to home
together, sweetly as one.

Thinking Back to Her

It's okay to let me go
for a moment to journey alone
to bear the torment once again,
but I promise I'll come home.

I have no fear of going back
just to reminisce,
a fleeting glance,
a word perchance,
or just an awkward kiss.

With all I'd note, I'd understand
that home is cradled in giving hands.
All we'd ever hope to see
is cloaked with self-discovery.

Every mistake I'd ever made
was a star placed in the sky,
traces left for the journey back
to the flickering home in your eyes.

And though it seems I'll walk away,
it's only then I'd see
all the tears I'd saved back then,
had I seen you walking toward me.

Star Stirrer

I wake in the small hours
to a sleepless dream
that walks over creaking floorboards.
It hardly believes itself, it seems,
and begs me for any proof,
but the owls are asleep high up on the branches.
My only company is
an awareness of you.

I leave words within millimeters
of your lips while you sleep,
and you'll not hear a breath.
But your heart will stir stars with its beat.

The Sentinel

To be a sentinel in the darkest
silence of your presence.
Soft release,
a mist of hope
inward drawn as essence.

So the breaths of lovers curl
in moonlight cast aglow,
melodic dreams to blend and purl,
a sweet diminuendo.

Wrapped in night, as you sleep,
soul stirs and comes untied
to lead your dreams to wander far,
my heart close by your side.

All the Love

All the love in the world we need
can be fit on the tip of a pin.
More than the bounty of earth, sky, and sea,
it would sooner get under our skin.

Bathing Angels

Were the angels there to gambol upon your heart
and laugh like sighs beneath seaside skies,
where stars blink on as I close my eyes,
waves curl over,
a heron flies,
and a crimson coast goes dark.

Were you here beside me when I thought I was alone,
running barefoot as the thermals cross
and took no heed if time were lost,
never wasted hope despite the cost.

I'd have promised if I'd known
that together we'd become a symphony,
for your heart beats like mine
and your exhale sounds like mine.
We've had oceans to sail on winds of time
with wounds and mountains in between.

Ambling in the surf in search of driftwood down the beach,
we spoke of dreams we'd forgotten, it seems,
while angels plucked on fragile strings,
fretting memories and failing schemes
to obtain things all along within our reach.

Gardens of Siam

Whiskers stir on dandelion stems
while dawn departs on fragrant winds.
"We see the sun; his shadow's falling,"
from the treetops cried the waling-waling.

Wink awake, oh dreaming rose.
Brush your trestles from the briers
'til the soils of your ancestral roots
and climb the trellis to all you aspire.

Your flowers await another day
to see how green his eyes.
Ruby hues will take their queues
from the orchids when they cry.

Dream and you'll hear a swinging gate
while working in your garden.
There past the fountain, you'll catch an image
of someone lost within.

You know this scented presence,
though its logic reveals little
until he steps into the garden
of long-awaited petals.

The orchids shout to the dandelions,
"Time to close up. It's after dark."
Two cool cats curl up to nap
in the cradle of an open heart.

Good-bye Greetings

I heard good-bye
whispered softly to my ear
through such sweet lips.
And I closed my eyes
so I didn't have to see her go,
waiting,
that such gentle a sound
would not carry very far into my heart.

That something that meant so much,
with such gravity,
could just go away forever
with a good-bye.

Everything,
once touched by time,
is forever part of us.
Good-bye does not undo
the greetings gone before.

It's harder to hear myself say it,
"Good-bye, my love."
See you later in my heart and my dreams
in the slight change in the tack of my sail.

The chip you made in the wine glass
is whatever left that differs,
only because you were once here.
It says the entire world
is unfinished business.

It Just Hurts

It just hurts.
Please give me
something cold to drink
or an ether to inhale
and reflect on as I sink.

Out on the vast sea of hope,
both bounty and debris
of shipwrecked dreams
drift in and out of reach
or possibility.

In views interceded by ocean swells,
he waded into rows of waves,
and the wind swarmed in to keep her company
there on the beach,
poised with grace.

The moon ascends from the horizon's edge,
casting light from the darkening east,
while the sun set in the shadows west,
burning up all within its reach.

Their breathing slowed, unfelt,
inaudible over the intertidal.
Not even the ocean could understand
the intimacy of this painful idyll.

Solemnity exists from beyond the dunes,
watching over the two silhouettes
looking out at an empty ocean.
We're different now,
but difference is but a sobriquet.
It's really the gift of pain's devotion.

***

A Goan beauty and I absconded to a beach in Florida. The clouds were
low and threatening, and the waves were churning. It was the first time she

saw me swim. She didn't come out into the water, but rather she sat and watched with knees pulled up to her chest, her mane of tresses blowing toward the north. The same person toppled the world.

Poetry is the language that connects her presence along beaches by the sea and the distant shores within my mind. There was no pain over what was lost, but rather for all that would never be found. As I wrote in *#25wtT*, "There's often less pain over all that is lost than there is for not at least once having some of what would never be found."

Alone

Alone, I create the perfect pose.
I'll sow a bounty of unheard prose.
So proud of my cups, so magnificent,
ornate, but filled with discontent.

We look for toads and kettle-bearers
and the quenching kiss of wayfarers,
who catch the drops of saccharin rain
in hand-formed vessels thrown from pain.

Love does not pour from Grecian urns,
but it is the absence in what we believe.
Embrace all you have and are able to give
than all you'd hope to receive.

The Light by Which You See You're Found

A forest black is felt more at night
than a forest seen by day.
Saplings of fear spring from the ground
toward the crown of the surrounding canopy.

Through the obsidian blackness,
a spire of moon glow arrives
to thread through limbs and flash within
our distant, wincing eyes.

The glint from a lunar reflection
is seen by another and lost again,
for by closing your eyes, you break the path
of light before reaching the other's ken.

Be shined upon so to shine upon
another in the shadows by which you're bound.
The lantern you carry finds them not;
rather it casts the light by which you're found.

The moon is love that floods in flames
through the heart of the darkened wood.
So your light will shine,
and there you'll find
yourself in the eyes of the beloved.

Mysteries Need Not Be Mysterious

You enter me through mysteries
and come to rest inside my heart,
like obsidian shadows from another soul
brushing gently along within me,
an untold intuition of who you are.

Softening luminescence,
you breathe a trail of nostalgic aromas
of honeysuckle and dew on the moss.
You glisten along the nexus
of a moment found after a moment's loss,
like pearls strung together
and touching sweetly,
clattering like chimes,
pattering a string of quiet satin kisses
that go on incompletely.

From distances beyond what may be measured,
with provenance in the tears of angels
on pillows of time,
I dream awake, entranced.
I enter you through mysteries
that cannot be seen, love blind.

And while bells don't ring,
it's clear to us.
They blend and blend and blend
to glow from brilliant eyes.
Low chimes sound like mysteries, not mysterious.
You're a strange fragrance on a familiar wind.

Rose Speak

The color and bloom of a breath when you speak,
I curl around every petal.
To see you as a daffodil
would only be to settle.

No, I think thou art a rose
in a garden rooted in love,
drawn deep down from a blood-red heart,
blessed by the cooing of a morning dove.

The Question to Your Answer

Love appears before we ask
to bless the future and heal the past.
Gleaming with wisdom of unspoken choices,
it patiently waits for the sounds of our voices.

It quells the fears of space and time,
forever onward, leaving no one behind.
From soft glowing eyes to flames of emotion,
melting horizons, and stirring the ocean,

it teases the mind into taking a leap,
emptying our breath, and filling dreams as we sleep.
It tricks the heart and draws a tear,
yet sweetly sings in the darkness of fear.

And though two paths may seem the same,
the journey of love will forever change,
shining one light on the rest of our lives.
The answer is knowing it always arrives.

***

I thought about ending this last stanza with "The answer will know when the question arrives."

Many a Season's Harvest

It was the autumn of our lives—
a breath, a breeze, a voice,
aging planks, and abandoned ploughs–
reaping options
and sowing a choice.

And so the logic is stressed
as one and one yields one
whether we stroll
or trudge in from the cold.
We arrive bountiful in a boundless home.

In a test of trust is a trace of rust,
trailing tears down a face of steel
with the sun angle's low.
I waited for snow,
pacing wish trails through a fallow field.

A kiss becomes the fabric
held together by seams of faith.
When winter is done
the foxes will run
softly in vernal equinox landscapes.

The earth turns in a moment beneath us
while the sparrow flies sweetly alone
past the larks
and into our hearts,
now empty where our crops had grown.

We'll gently cast seeds along furrows
through summer-warmed soils at sunset,
safe in the ground
to emerge with a sound
of a choir that brings in our harvest.

The Messenger

I slip an arrow from the quiver.
Oh, last messenger, please deliver
this note I've written from my heart.
And without which, I'm only part.

I licked the feathers, drew the bow,
closed my eyes, and let it go.

I hear the fibers resonate,
a gentle sound for such a fate.

Point, then shaft, then feathers fly,
An arc of hope across the sky.

I open my eyes but lose its sight,
a glowing arrow in waning light.

Wishing all its time aloft,
I'm unaware the note slips off.

Falling gently through the air,
it softly finds an archer standing there.

Drawing arrow and preening feather,
she pauses and begins to read the letter.

A kiss of words hushes the shiver,
so she returns her arrow to its quiver.

In her heart, she bears the note,
while my heart longs for what it wrote.

Oh, messenger, please hear my prayer.
Return my note with an archer's care.

Three Minutes and Thirty-Nine Seconds

Two lives pirouette in a pristine moment,
slipping by the sentries of time.
If all were dark, one star and one spark,
would inspire their hopes to align.

A quarter moon floats in the Northern Lights
so many years ago,
lighting her path for a wayfarer,
but not this body, as so.

His pen hastens echoes in silence,
and for her, there are no words and no need.
His every sentence an hour asks,
"Why sooner can't it be?"

Souls spin dreams at their nexus.
Hearts and minds do not forget.
The sound of a voice calls them home,
'tis mute and softly desperate.

Facing paths of thorns, fire, and rock,
mountains along the way
gather forever to fill the void
of an instant held at bay.

Her eyes are liquid constellations.
His words are steps they start to climb,
steady and knowing,
like diamonds and garnets
to forever remember this time.

The sunrise pulls them in weightless,
free and one in the other's presence.
Her eyes fill the void of a lifetime
in three minutes and thirty-nine seconds.

In the Literal Zone

The precious chance for a lonely thought loose
slips and fades sinuously free,
a melodious stream of nostalgic mist
off an Arabica sea.

Curiously exhaled from dissonance
in an amber-lit café,
he imagines himself a sojourner,
a wayfarer without a way.

Longshore drifts en echelon.
Long minutes march by metronome.
Long is the spellbound beachcomber
for an island all his own.

Long is the dream of an inland man,
lost to his seaside girl.
There's a diver down where the standard waves
swimming dizzy for a polished pearl.

Light from her eyes plays on sea glass chips,
tumbling in the curling waves
that crest and break on a beach that waits
for a wish he once had made.

The surf is heard like a lingering kiss,
breathing ripples on the smoothening sand.
And just as the whisper and simmering fades,
Another promise swells, tumbles, and lands.

The ocean is love running breathless
in a race between the moon and the sun,
causing tides to surge across the poignant curve
of an incandescent blue horizon.

A tranquil star contracts and bursts
in pulsing neon spires.
There's forever a star expiring
while life glows like embers in the fire.

If this writer could paint, it would be a portrait
of the empty space next to him,
awaiting the image of a seagoing girl
dancing waves on a canvas of ocean.

Lines in the Sand

Sleepy words awaken
Like a stirred morning child,
Wincing through lashes at clarity
Betwixt dreams and noises outside.

They skip through their days,
Slipping from grasp
Of convention, imagination,
And institution, alas.

Like clay, paper, and notes,
They become idle matter for craft
Until love cast the canvas.
They're artists at last.

As sketches and phrases
Lift illusion from pages,
They carve blocks of hope,
Soulful forms, tall and ageless.

Love's art, once feared,
Had slipped through their hands
To reappear as simple, golden
Soft lines in the sand.

Wounded Poetry

Like a once-broken promise, she came to me
out of my past, across forever seas,
casting her truth into the furrows of dreams,
sowing intimate seeds that hushed the screams.

And these unsolved riddles of throttling fear.
that one day next, hope would not get here,
disappearing in the swells so far from land,
with spice scents, driftwood, and contraband.

Like caramel drippings from a Dali sun,
her eyes cast colors on taut sails of muslin.
She falls sweet and softly through scents and caresses,
like settling snowflakes on dried winter branches.

She is more than a feeling, brighter than sight.
She is the stir in the morning to my withering night.
And I recall her breath from a fathomless deep,
landing home in my heart from a precipitous leap.

But the bitter serenity when out of my sight
is her touch to my soul like raw senses at night.
I spiral away; she'll not get here in time
to keep me from falling deeper in mind.

In this strange, numb world, it's just her and me,
afloat on the tears of wounded poetry.

Seasoning

If silence and solitude were to have weight,
they'd flower these hills, held fast in place,
which draw a chill from this glaucous sky
into fleeting cold winds, pulling tears from my eyes.

Chimney smoke mingles above the rooftops
and can be smelled across empty playground lots.
A stolid chill dons a winter's dusk shroud,
as the sun slips away behind dull, distant clouds.

As they stew over secret recipes,
these families are conjuring remedies
that season more deeply in winter's love.
So thicker runs the courses of blood.

Bare tree limbs reach up like dead hands on a clock,
near a merry-go-round hunkered down in bedrock.
Ruts from the rails of a Radio Flyer
trail a lone child's footprints, both frozen with mire.

As I shiver alone in my questioning state,
unsecured and open swings a gate.
From unseen origins they fall from the sky,
these snowflakes that soften with tears in my eyes.

I'm not sure if ever or otherwise when
our journeys will deliver us, convergent friends.
But the lessons we harvest from each season's end
make for savory spices when the next one begins.

Love and the Itinerant Lover

It doesn't fail.
It always leads us by the hand,
faster and faster,
pinching into the folds of night.
And we let it slip through our fingers
and watch it run ahead,
disappearing in the darkness,
leaving us itinerant
under an obsidian sky.

Flesh

Earth pulls up its collar as the sun sets.
All things cooling creak.
The quietest is flesh.

Pouring life through the waist of leaded glass,
countless grains, two souls, are in the talus
as fabrics glide, fiber, and mesh,
warmth and velvet.
The softest is flesh.

Peeling layers of life, the mist from the rind,
freed and immortal, sprays silent and fine,
sweet to the palette, nostalgic breaths
fueled by scent.
The most fragrant is flesh.

A grape on a vine in the rain, dew, and brine,
sea fog through vineyards, is a portrait of time.
My words are as fleeting as love is endless,
as lost as Latin.
The most seen is flesh.

You elude the patter of fingers on keys.
Uncloaking the letters shows a poet's disease.
Swirling in air, our winter breaths
are warmed by our mouths.
The most tasted is flesh.

Of all the senses most fathomless
and least endeared,
you are my now,
my forever,
my flesh.

Tree Rings

Our moments collect in concentric rings
about the nexus
of a first embrace adorned with
autumnal colors and scents.

We lovers blend,
cupped gently below
the stir of flecks and dapple.
Each leaf high up quivers in the bouquets
and knows when to let go,
fly, and fall to earth.

Whispers from a rustling canopy climb
down the bark encasements
of these tall and somnolent trees.
Thirsty, brilliant leaves,
which clatter and kiss,
wink awake, hold our gaze, and
suspend our hearts.

In a pirouette amidst
the amity of recollection and premonition,
we shimmer in an iridescence
of saffron on copper.
Beloved, remember this?

Moments light up,
each one for just an instant,
the last of our lives,
each conveniently the beginning
of forever and forever smiles
at us.

Rippling across the cycles of solstice and equinox,
we radiate,
a nostalgic procession toward unmade memories,
like tree rings.
We fly and fall in love.

The Ballerina

Her world is wound by latency,
an arc of a dancer waiting to be,
expressions of something beyond herself,
a single spring flowing toward someplace else.

The beauty of change leaves illusive effects
at the very same moment she leaps into the next.

Love Is the Finest Form of Dying

There is a thin fine line between giving up on yourself
and giving up on needing another,
between striving for that spring green flexibility
and tormenting ourselves when we bend in the slightest way
in the slightest breeze.

The hollowing pain rips through our torso,
like seething heavy balls shot from distant black pig iron cannons,
like when love unbridled goes careening into boundless plains before
it can be tamed,
and yet how we hang on to it until we become the wild ones.

Love has a place, and that place is in our hearts,
where it stays and loops in lemniscates of infinity.
It doesn't go out to others;
rather they enter into our hearts.

Until it all becomes an indistinguishable melt within us,
still, like idiot savants,
we squint, study, and analyze our philosophies in dialectics
with beautiful wayfarers and vigilant family,
giving friends and torrid lovers.
And we get confused, sad, and then more sad,
thriving on it, thumping like heartbeats.

Until sadness becomes as delicate and fragile as angel hair,
like fine capillaries at the distant edge of tree roots,
not even those to anchor us anymore to the earth.

I am certain now that my love is not out there.
Even the hunch I once had that she was is gone,
for she is already inside me,
as the pause in my pulse.

She is so entwined with the syncopated rhythms of my breath
that I cannot even distinguish her anymore,
so I shed my understanding of love.
I give up the search and drop my implements and defenses.
I will squander my love to others, as I have for so long,
and be happy that I can express at all.

Pierced by spires of joy, dripping with tears,
now I know within there is an endless supply of both,
love and tears.

Bring on the parade of mistakes,
and I will curse and scream out my love
until I lose my voice when I can be madly certain
no one can hear me.

Where my eyes next frost over with saline,
the last streak of glitter rolls to a stop on my cheek,
and then I think there I shall die.

Chapter 2

Whispers of a Silent Heart
(Khamosh Dil ki Sarghoshiyan)

Agzikarahan Caravanserai, Cappadocia, 2013

Introduction

In your life, there might have been a moment of self-reflection where you found yourself in an immutable state of "Whoa!" Or perhaps you found nothing. Even now you might be looking both deeply inward and all around you, struggling for a purpose while everything happening in this space and time is blindly evolving and terminable. You may be standing amidst people, places, and events that are all washing waves of change upon the shores of your life. Who you are, your purpose, and meaning each arc across the universe in search of something. All of these present your depth and breadth of value to others, yourself, and the Divine. This state of tender questioning is the origin of these poems, largely written over the past twenty-eight months while under the influence of something that can only be described as divine. Some of us are always under this influence, but we should be delicate in how we define "divine," for every idea and every fleeting thought about it seems to drift beyond linguistic containment. Consciousness is within us, yet something about it defies logic and delimitation. There is a universe within you. Its magnificent emptiness provides for the expansion of consciousness, creativity and the awareness of some unfathomable meaning that is both within what is known and beyond what is unknown.

Chances are, you are undergoing an evolution of self during a revolution of circumstances. This can easily flip, and suddenly you are amidst a revolution, and you must gingerly evolve through what you gather from the rigor of your surroundings. This poetry reflects paradigmatic, seismic, and cathartic shifts in self-realization, external awareness, presence and the resulting actions.

This chapter is not about what love is, but that it just *is*. Love is *is*. It is not *a was*, nor a *to be*. *Is* is the indescribable and unknowable yet absolute state that can only be approximated through the illusion of what *absoluteness* might be. It is love as the connective state of all that does and does not exist. *Is* encompasses both our elusive sense of divine reality and limited senses of our manifested being. *"Love is"* connects I with you and God with me. Love connects the sinner to the savior and the student to the teacher. A deep love for another human being can transcend to such an extent as to decouple the lover from the object of love so that neither exist and there is just *love*. In these states, love rises from below the glowing embers of your identity and burns brighter than anyone could endure on this plane of existence. This poetry carries some solemnity as love itself consumes both the lover and beloved in flames of gnosis. It attempts to cast a faint spell in which we transcend from *we are* to *I am* to *God is*.

The poems are heavy in mystical explorations of self, soul and spirit and are flavored by deep explorations of Sufism or a personalized extension of philosophical studies and other ontological jaunts over the past few decades. I am just a poet and by no means an expert or guru, sheikh or murshid, shaman or mentor, or anyone else you might need in order to find your way into yourself.

I make frequent references to God and scriptural and mythical characters who either directly shape or metaphorically reflect human consciousness and divine nature. Some references are presented through a variety of linguistic expressions with etymological roots in Arabic, Urdu, Persian, Turkish, and Sufism. But again I'm just a poet flirting with scholarly fantasy. This is a spiritual read if you are a spiritualist, a religious read if you are a religionist, or a philosophical read if you are a philosopher. I expect you will read these poems through your own personal filters; although I prefer to think of them less as filters than as predispositions, fluxing states of being, and inspired inclinations. The latter are free to change through the dissolution of filters, biases, and veils.

I present both obvious and subtle metaphors in hopes of provoking new perspectives and unifying a vicissitude of meaning within the reader. I often write under the influence of something beyond my own direct understanding (auto-writing), and like you, I have to sort it out afterward. I am sometimes asked for the meaning of a specific poem, but I often find myself answering by writing yet another poem. It's a spiraling conundrum. It's better to read and listen to yourself … and not ask me.

The poems are not in any particular sequence, and I attempt to break up the more intense with equally meaningful and more playful poems, such as "I Followed a Writer Up a Tree," "Abandoned by Youth," "Somnolescence," and "Written." Many are what I call "black sky poems," intended to open an empty dark night sky for you to fill in with your own stars, planets, and moons or clouds and flaming arrows. A poem is intended to lift the latch on the gates of the imagination and self-disclosure and then stand back as readers burst out into the boundless fields of personal interpretation, the heaven of poetry.

My dear friend Arshia Qassim wrote about this chapter,

> "I often find my own dilemma of in-distinction between worldly love and divine love echoed in the words of Skip's poems. It evades factual explanation that flesh and soul are so closely intertwined like the double helices of DNA. One strand would be insufficient to sustain life. And similarly, it is in the rungs joining these two strands where love jumps from one to another and constitutes this amazing body spirit conglomeration. He describes this beautifully in his writings, and while it is comforting and reassuring on one level, it is infuriating at another, because of its inherent futility in worldly terms. Yet one cannot escape the transcendence this perspective confers."[6]

---

[6] Arshia Qassim, Letters to the Poet, 2016

Entered a Dervish

Her heart's smoke rose
from doused flames of love.
Wisps entwined with her obsidian tresses
remain interwoven with gray
and a long journey's dust.

From the door she entered there went
a whirling dervish whose time was spent
amidst a rose whose petals red
was just her reflection iridescent.

Two lovers met at a karmic juncture.
Their purpose remained unknown to the other.
At the peak of their love,
these beloved friends
were called home by their Master
and whirled to their end.

Oh, Icarus, What Have You Done?

Up here, hollering winds unsettle the dust
softening on Empyrean.
Rising thermals graze cloud meadows.
Up here, those who dress in shadows
dare not enter dreams of men.

Upon my brow, this nimbus glows.
Bestowed on my ascent,
I bow in flight
on wings wraithlike,
eschewing the day to chase the night
in bolts across the firmament.

Surrender brings lightness to a leaf
Behold my feather, the freer's blade.
Time is but its morrow's thief,
a bounty box of verdant leaves
released before the ransom's paid.

Oh, Icarus, what have you done?
Our escape was not your calling.
Through life we sleep and death we rise,
yet vanity undreamt your vaster skies
into an ocean, woken, falling.

Speaking Love into the Shadows

Arshia Qassim, Artist

She spoke of love immodestly,
reciting inscriptions on poesy rings.

He spoke of love as poets do.
Not one vivid word did she eschew.

Others summoned God as judge and witness,
each one sure his description fittest.

Then one amidst our conversation
stirred quietly from his meditation.

Lifting his face and opening his eyes,
he spoke to each and all's surprise.

"I've listened for love in all you say,
and with every name, you chased it away.

So I followed its path in silent prayer.
Where it led, I could not care.

And there I found 'twas me love sought,
not me for it, whose name is naught."

Crossing the Bosphorus

There is a place where redolent memories sway
on the winds arriving from yesterday,
from Remeli across to the Anadolu Feneri
and through the Bosphorus from Marmara to the Black Sea.

Voluminous vessels cross this strait
with treasured scents for a cargo of fate,
landing none too early and none too late,
just in time to empty the weight
of thoughts on the shores of moments like this
that receive the waves that reminisce
His ninety-nine names or the One we seek.
All truths reside in the heart we keep.

***

    True events inspired this poem, which describes a most fortunate journey across the Bosphorus while visiting Istanbul. Sometimes when you are called to enter the tavern of love, all modes of transportation appear. It was truly a miracle that I was present on this day, that is, when I was the companion of a seeker who ripened, was plucked from the vine, and gently became the wine.

The Garden Road

Nourished by love for the unseen within,
when seen by a heart,
it shimmers sans end.

Swells the bud,
a flame before bloom,
sans thorn,
sans pain,
sans sojourner's wound.

The wilting,
the dying,
the falling to earth,
the paradox is wrapped in a gift of rebirth.

In death, so many nod in decay
whose hues loved light until light loved gray.
Deep-hearted thinker, let loose the reins
to careen through redolent gardens again.

Pause a moment on a fragranced path.
You'll hear a subtle message splash.
'Tis a tear of Mercury's reflection,
reciting, "Whence you came is where you go.
Take heed. All roads
but One direction."

Unfree Poem

Diana Matisz, Photographer, Artist

A poem is a bird
in a gilded cage,
a pining soul
on a weeping page.

Open the door
but still it stays.
Close the door,
and it flies away.

I Followed a Writer Up a Tree

I followed a writer
up a prodigious tree,
every leaf I brushed
his poem.

From the crown,
I scanned the pastoral,
a poetic landscape in repose,
a resplendent chorus of
glistening verdant wisdom.

O vast vibrato of sibilance
slipping the breaths of
Thalia and Melpomene!
Alight by dusk, I lingered.

Now comes the long wind of winter
to undress each tree.
So from my aerie,
through gaunt branches,
I could a changing see.

From the low-slung place
where each poem fell.
I thought, "Here so many,
clothed in so much comedy
and tragedy
recite their odes
of heaven and hell."

And down I climbed,
and away I walked
over quiescent leaves
while red and russet
ran from their dendritic veins,
moldering into the palette
of dormant memories.

O even now,
the sweet scent of decay
reminds me of spring,
when I will climb again
from the rot of the roost
to the dust below boots.
By the pen of the winter writer,
spring will come again.

Sword and Dagger

I sat with God in supplication
before the sun rose this morning
and bared my chest
to offer a life in exchange for a heart.

He took the dagger from my one hand
and put a sword in the other.
This is how He saves and takes a life.

Seamless with Light

Only beauty grows from this visceral ache,
like a seed pushing up through the earth of your chest.

Once a heart takes root within the abyss of the self,
multihued flowers lift high in the welkin.

The pain of the water that courses through shadows
splits strata of rock to find stark verdant meadows.

Love for grief, like wind, raises the flame,
stealing air from filled lungs 'til we're steady again.

As each thread is woven to make a fine fabric,
if one is missed, 'tis nothing so tragic.

But if after the cloth is finished, then worn
by one thread removed, into two it is torn.

There's as much hurt in fortune as wisdom in plight.
Embrace both, for your darkness is seamless with light.

Sans Words

Sans a single word
printed within the voluminous corpus of epic poetry,
their unrevealed meaning
would flow beyond
the endless rows of bookshelves
that hold their parchment.

We are forever mending the mew with words
while the mystery within attempts to escape the mind
and take solace in the haven of the heart.

Gaze silently, for one quiet candle
can consume a thousand suns
and be blown out by a single pair of lips.

Colors of Love

Love is a prism,
a translucent gem,
a refractor of futures,
and remember whens.

Divine light enters,
and there it bends
the monochromaticity
of every man.

Fans in gradations,
spectacular hues
as love fills the palette
from which to choose
all of the spectrum
for the heart to blend
His ninety-nine colors
into white light again.

Seeking Love

Seeking love
is chasing the setting sun around the earth,
pleading for it to rise again.

Be still.
Turn and wait.
It will come.

Orbit yourself.
You will become the east and the west
within which love becomes your axis.

Ishq, the Sun and the Moon

"Water derives its color from the vessel that holds it."
Sufi Al-Junaid of Baghdad

Behold the Moon, she loves the Sun so deeply
that all we see of her
is the solar light of her beloved
reflecting off her lunar surface,
otherwise dark and invisible.

How pleased the Sun must be
to behold such a blushing beauty,
to know that of himself,
his own disclosure
manifested within another
so supplicant
as his Moon.

With such burgeoning love,
all the Moon comes to know of herself
is the source that fulfills its desire,
which blushes her cheeks.

Thus, the Sun and Moon
become indistinguishable
in the shared singular light,
mirror images,
each mirroring the other.

The Moon speaks,
"What else can I be
but the reflection of my Beloved?
What else then is my Beloved
besides that which illuminates
my own heart's essence?"

So the Divine One
presented humans with the cosmos
so their hearts might look up and observe
these celestial bodies
and take lesson.

What I see within the heart of another
is my heart looking into itself.
It is God's *plan of reflection* that two thus exist
so God's pure light
is reflected in and by both.

A vision of oneself
with the psycho-physical faculties of oneself
is a state of solitude
and attribute of aloneness.
It is meditative gnosis of self.

When the place of vision is shifted
through the presence of another,
their relationship itself
fulfills the archetype of that union we seek with
God.

The conjoined reflection itself
finds a deeper state of solitude
within the nexus of a placeless place.
And this nexus is in the heart.

So what of the Moon and the Sun themselves
in their solitude.
How do they reconcile
divine and human love?

From gnosis of self,
the seeker within the lover
moves toward gnosis of universe
and then gnosis of God.

"From Ghanood to Adraak
to immersive Warood
and then Kashaf,
a key turns
Fatah of Shahood
and then fana al fana
toward fana fillah,
silent
AllaHu
wa Baqaa billah."

As the gaze of
the supplicant lover
and the beheld beloved
volley in the same light between them,
their love for the other
ponders the archetype of there being *no* other.

Who then to love if the Sun and Moon become one?
How are they to be *none other* to each other
if there is no *other*?

So begins the *haj* and *jihad* between
Ishq-majazi (love of God's creation) and *Ishq-haqiqi* (love of truth).
The Moon and Sun seek *haqiqi* with none other but God,
but embrace within *majazi* for no other but each other.

Can the Moon and Sun unite
to dissolve their otherness?
Or does the annihilation of self (other) in *majazi*
become idolatrous?

Perhaps the Sun and Moon
are alone as one with each other
but One Alone In God.

Nothing can be more truthful
than beholding with the heart
that which cannot be seen with the eyes.

It is God's indescribable light
streaming through.

Words Form a Trail

Words leave a trail
laid by the vain wandering of a mind
tormented by an unheard heart,
sure and silent signs
that can never be followed
back to where their meaning starts.

Pure light hurtles through the cosmos,
seeking certain intersections
that reflect a latent essence,
approximating absolutes
observed in relative dimensions
where kindled lovers kiss and catch fire
before one's intention
quenches the other's desire
were mind and heart to each conspire
over the sweet resin within the aloes-wood.

Oh, they'd be one
of unspeakable meaning
that begets a word
no sooner spoken
before ever that word
is understood.

Not to Be Withheld

A love cannot be withheld
that is not purely ours to give.
So the hollowed reed
filled by the breath of the Divine
makes the sweetest sound.

Love is a musician
that cannot help but play
God's composition
for the Beloved only to listen.

If thirsting,
we should love the depths
of even the shallowest river,
for in that bed
grows the uncut reed that quenches.

Love with Nothing: Why Be a Prism?

When someone gives you more
than you could imagine giving yourself,
it's God's ever-presence,
showing you the bounty of your own heart.

It is divine discloser. It is
the paradox, that all you never needed,
has been in your heart
before the dawn of existence.

The conundrum of divine love
is made complex by human faculties
designed through habit
to work only on complexity.

Why be a prism to white light
when you can be translucent?
The most important instrument you have
is nothing.

Pawns of Pronouns

In "I love you,"
who is *I*,
and who is *You*?
For *love* is the bridge
between them.

Their distinction is a mystery
by which *I*
discloses within *You*
and *You*
within *I*.

I've crossed over many a mystery,
only to find myself
waiting on the other side.

Words are not of the heart,
nor the mind,
but a bridge between.

Falling Out of Love and Into Truth

Bed-bound and solitudinous,
out beyond the edge of reason,
beyond where my senses can claim,
I cannot sleep, wake, or dream,
a state of insouciant stillness
bereft of unnecessary memories.

I am not loved.
I do not love
in ways I can no longer understand.

Stark states of stalemate,
Melpomene and Thalia
remain hunched over game pieces
of a drunken heart,
lamenting all a sober mind must reason.

When liquid gold and golden light
take to loving,
we as humans are no match.

Either of these elixirs
in their limpidness
bronzes our throat,
smothers our breath,
and consumes our vision.

Lingering on the last
still drift of sulfur struck,
my flickering writhe
is a lambent match flame
leaning in
to kiss a wild bonfire.

Come Hither in the Silence

Silence blossoms
while mere words wither
in empty spaces,
echoing,
calling,
"Beloved, come hither."

A flower knows not
for whom its petals show,
yet its fragrance
seems so personal
as if meant for me alone.

What Is Forgotten

What is forgotten is easily replaced.
All else remains divine.
Quiet rings of ripples last
long after the Beloved's pebble is cast
to vanish beneath the water line.

From self's still axis,
a deeper message is heard
in the silence
between the echo,
rising in the azure sky
on the thermal's rise,
where prayers go.

A deluge of words
wash against the ears
yet not a drop to quench the drought
or bathe away salt-crystal tears.

Soundless is the river's drift
that carries us
through parted lips
home to harvest
the black fruit orchards
dotting the red-walled fields
where the divine rain falls
so a fertile heart yields.

Where it's buried
cracks the seed
to grow and ripen on the vine,
then plucked and pressed,
and poured in cup,
then further ripens
in the drunkard's mind.

***

If something necessitates its own forgetting—if it's truly that fundamental, material, and capable of decay and it can erode and break down within your mind, it's clearly something of a kind that can be surpassed and replaced by something else. It's a pity, but it happens. But something might reign beyond the replaceable. Its foundation's essence is deeply rooted in your heart. It may be that the object lost may have only at first come to remind you of the presence of its spirit, which persists within.

In this poem, the black fruits might be olives or grapes. The distinction is likely moot, or the metaphor might be a beloved or object of affection. The intoxication (the spirit) isn't in the grape or wine, but it's in the heart of the drunkard. This is a Sufi love poem, and its meaning can be further explored throughout this chapter.

To expand on this topic, that which we think we become, we already were. Where is the sweetness of the chocolate? Is it within the chocolate? Is it on the tongue or in the mind? How is it that the pleasantness of sweetness, aside from the food, is recollected and welcomed among the category of all things sweet? The sweetness is within you, awaiting whatever sensory awareness that will bring about its cognizance.

Likewise, the bitterness is within you too, also awaiting. The "ness" of everything is within everything, as it was commanded "to be" in pre-eternity (a term to refer to timelessness and spacelessness). One might say the same for love persisting beyond both before and after its object. The essence of love (love-ness) is in you already. It doesn't arrive; it doesn't depart.

So of what practical use is this discussion? Once we attach our immersion in love to an external (for example, another person), there is an illusion that, when the external goes, we are without love, that is, somehow love has let us down or eluded us. There is a sense that the most important universal concept of love now has to be found somewhere or with someone else. But our attachment to the external, not the external itself, lets us down. The love, like the alleged sweetness of the chocolate and intoxication in the bottle, is already within us. We are already everything within ourselves, waiting to become cognized again. If you look into your deepening states of awareness, you can taste sweetness without a chocolate, become intoxicated without the wine, and feel love in moments of detached solitude without the beloved's touch or memory.

The alcoholic despairs that he has lost his ability be happy without his bottle. The glutton despairs that he cannot know sweetness enough without more candy. The lover despairs that the feeling of true love is not achievable without someone to attach to. I am a drunkard who slakes his addictions by sipping from the eclectic flask of his own heart.

Abandoned by Youth

There are those with whom
we are only meant to share
silence.

He, a single bead of dew,
aged well,
yet threadbare.

Clung to the cat tongue edge of a
green blade of grass,
she, a daughter among the olive trees,
has the olive in her palm,
cured at the bottom of his glass.

We are all to become done,
and what's done
is done though
its purpose
has not passed.

With each dream, a hair
fell from the head.
'Tis the silence in falling
that wakes one from dreams
instead.

These *men gone missing*
from lost souls
kissing
have been found
by authorities.

Beckoned from behind the veil,
they came along
quietly, quietly,
thirsting love and flesh
and frail.

"Your soul is but a diamond's shine,"
said the smiling sage.
"Abandoned by youth,
lost in the dunes,
and found
in the sands through the vision of age."

Teach You to Fly

Look at the reflections
of cloud and sky
and beautiful landscapes
that shine in your eyes.

Wings open inward
to a world inside
from here in your heart.
I'll teach you to fly.

Iqra (Recite)

That which is defined
within a pristine cognition
before the utterance of its word
is a metaphor, an approximation.
All this wordless pondering
is a paradox
for those silent and wandering.

The spiritual distance is unlocked
that is secretly sealed
between the word of revelation
and the revelation thus revealed—
but not by he who wields the pen,
for he does not control the writing.
Rather 'tis the one who listens to the inspiration
who controls the meaning in the tidings.

The path from the heart
to the writing hand
and the speaking lips
is fraught with struggle in between
the ego and the intellect.
The truth is a negotiation
by spiritual dialectic,
the alchemy of meaning
within the science of our sohbet.

We're bid to recite through drawn veils
woven thick,
yet whose translucency
shows the filament of self-disclosure
glowing bright with the heart's sagacity,
inspired messages scripted
for those with vision beyond what's seen.

Now comes a soft wind from a voice
blowing dust off the cover to a book
written pre-eternity.
Truth is as quiet and vacuous
as any man can bare
from depths recited painfully.

The trial for the messenger,
whose enlightenment we seek,
the purpose for which his message sown,
is to become the poetry within the poems
that the beleaguered poet speaks.

Writing the Way Home

Ricochet shreds skin.
Shattered marbles are shot by
childish thoughts at play
from a circle etched by a blunted knife
into the hardened dirt
of a playground,
paved for life,
weaving threads of clarity
to patch the weary fabric of
a garment made of poetry,
real people, drama, and pageantry,
all turned like pages never-ending.

But love holds the hand
that holds the pen
that writes
poignant poems
where even the homeless
find a home
wherever the writer can.

An Earth candy piñata wrapped in parchment,
scribbled with sonnets,
couplets, and quatrains
for bat-armed readers
and sweet-toothed beaters
swinging at iambic whatever-meter.

Poetry is the ancient press
for the records of humanity,
who drags its demons, ghosts, and fairies
from open graves in cemeteries.

These life's dark tunnels through the heart,
seekers of light, endeavor to plod,
relighting the torch as the flame gets colder,
carrying life's scripture on heavy shoulders
to deliver their bounty to God.

Abandon Everything

Both our angels,
dark and light,
come out by dawn or dusk,
under cover of night,
carrying torches when the body's cold.

With palm leaves for shade
in the heart's abode,
not a brick is laid
to reinforce high walls.
Ere I've torn them down.
No one ascends from earth to empyrean,
trading his burden pound for pound.

Abandon everything
that belongs below ground.
My love has no handles.
Your love has no hands.
Raise your voice
without making a sound.

The chill behind you
that shudders your chest
is the breath of the Beloved,
breathing life into death.

In Vino Veritas

Do not seek revelation in one event.
Rather draw inward the sum of your experience.
Then exhale
to blow them away like a fine powder
into the abyss of space.

In empty, drunken dissolution,
the unspeakable, unhearable happens.
Your message finds you in the inhale,
and for a moment,
nothing moves.

Harken unto your inner voice.
The next words you speak
are truth.

Damascene Sword

You're too used to your blunted ways.
Worn habits of reason is why you stay.

You're so tired of hearing the same arcane
lines from a heart cashing in on pain.

Grab your Sufi-sluicing pan.
Ya, Allah, let's pull the gold of soul by hand.

From this parched and grinning desert creek
sift the dust and graveled speech.

Unlearn the ways you understood.
Mine the vein; the pay is good.

Trade the bone china we can't afford
for tin cans, wool, and a Damascene sword.

Love Is a Steady Wind

Love is a steady wind
that erases what we know of it
as soon as we try to grasp.

It is pre-eternal wisdom,
named by God
within the heart,
a whisper.

A feather softly landed.
Let it lie.
'Tis an attribute of another name,
eternal light,
not intermittent flame.

When called through lips,
a sound a kiss became.
When a breath says "love,"
it's lost to winds,
only to land
if it flies again.

Of this fierce glow
that Love and You
within my breast inspire,
the Sun is but a spark that flew
and set the heavens afire.

Broad-Shouldered Lions

Broad-shouldered lions
stand over the ocean's quietude,
roaring thunder in the surf,
thudding sand-laden questions
with salt-soaked and matted paws
and fathomless eyes of intention.

Surly supplicants beseech the sea,
whose tides answer only to the sun and moon.
A lion's home is the African veldt,
so go home, King of Hearts.

The seekers lead; the answers follow.
And within the question, they find their start.

Words Are Rolling Stones

Words are rolling stones
that clatter in the stream of time.
Any of we, parched or quenched,
sip at the water's edge and listen to them,
purling and purling, sublime
'til their edges rounded by translation
turn rock to sand, like grapes to wine.

Precise words of ancient mystics
over river falls then out to sea they flow.
Who can ever say anything for sure about
a mystic, who himself asks,
"Who is He who says words with my mouth?" (Rumi)

Let's never lose sight of the poetry
through the veil of a poem that's so pronounced.
Maulana is a single breeze
carrying a multitude of scents.
Sensual words are metaphors for meaning
that are they themselves
metaphors for sensuality,
names within names
for a singularity.

There is only one pure text,
and each of us solely hears its truth.
It is written on the walls of the heart.
In strokes of blood, there in the dark,
its mystery is its only proof.

Poison on the Arrow's Point

The only truth is the one I choose
and choose and choose.
What then of these arrows
dipped in the elixir of delusion
and sent forth by the bow of truth?

Love may go awry,
but the archer always makes his mark.
We'll sooner die from bleeding than
from the poison on the arrow's point.
The universal adhesive for pairs who seek to be one
is in whether each can endure being two.

Sparrow Eats the World

If I knew who I'd be
by the last line of this poem

If I knew who'd sway, besotted, beside me
to lean in and catch the last word
of our maundering sohbet[7].

If this, I'd never have left
my Beloved's company to begin with.
I crawled wild-eyed from the depths
of the inexplicable,
cold embers of abandoned age,
to go there,
to go to the tip
where the flame flickers
and breath burns.
The Beloved is the earth,
my awareness, roots.

If this,
then love is the water
flowing through the rock,
drawn up the vine
to fatten the grape.

This drunken dance
is a fruit harvest.
We fools are the wine makers.
Who gets who intoxicated?

Bestami Bayazid said,
"I am the wine drinker and the wine and the cupbearer
I came for from Bayazid-ness as a snake from its skin.
Then I looked and saw that lover and beloved are one
I was the smith of my own self.
I am the throne and the footstool.
Your obedience to me greater than my obedience to you

---

[7] Sohbet is a Turkish word for deep listening and discussion at often mystical
levels and states.

I am the well-preserved tablet.
I saw the Kaaba walking around me."

I say
I arrived in this place one thousand sunsets back
but had only to travel from mind to heart to get here.
The earth makes its way around the sun on my behalf.
My journey is both a somber desert
and a purling rain forest.
It is the pause of the ego
that makes one or the other so.

A hungry sparrow hops cautiously through bread crumbs
strewn around a fat, stale loaf of bread.
The feast is on the table;
our hands are in our pockets;
our mouths are sealed shut.
With bellies full of hesitation, we circle about the spread.
Empty are the stores of those who
will sate their hunger for truth.
The sparrow with an empty belly
sees the universe in a morsel of bread.
So of what use is the whole loaf?

The Secret of the Heart (Qalb)

This poem dons the thorny cloak of consequence.
Readers listen for its truth, but only the truthful hear.

Life is a kiss, a soft touch, else the prick from the thorn of a rose.
Seek love through beauty, but do not trample in gardens of idols.

From the mysterious combustibles of the heart,
true love smolders in the eyes of the friend.

Our babbling into oblivion leaves us in rented repose.
Friends made to bide the commands of their heart.

They are meant to wake along the sun's blue arc of horizon.
Stirred by fleeing zephyrs, our dreams rise fast on their heels.

God wakes not the dreamers with wordless hearts,
whose flagons fill with love to overflow reality's cup.

Those delivered from God are left to love others,
to dream awake and not wander off on winged words.

Oh, as my consciousness slips away in silence,
my lips spin silk into wildly flailing ribbons of flame.

God seals the scent of truth in my heart
and calls the faithful opener to draw the fiery bow.

We who glow like embers are also shadows cast by light,
just as the moon is a phantom without the sun.

As it reflects the sun, it casts light as if its own.
If not mirrors in each other's sky, what truth and beauty shown?

For each step taken toward God, He takes ten toward us.
How am I to love a lover like that?

Nothing among everything and everything among nothing.
"Where shall I go from thy presence when thou art everywhere."

'Tis the prismatic heart of the poet alchemist
that frees the noble metal from its base alloy.

But my Beloved casts a white light no prism breaks.
'Tis no colorful shards to speak and none to replicate.

Love is pre-eternal wisdom, named by God,
whispered into the heart, and sealed by silence.

A secret unlocked with the lips flies away untold.
The key lies within the unopened vessel of truth.

It is you who are being unlocked by it.
Your passage to the *qalb* is your annihilation.

Our gift of truth is unwrapped from the inside from the heart.
It ascends through dying bone and sinew.

***

Qalb is Arabic that literally translates to "heart," but it is beyond just the organ. *Qalb* is more "essence of heart" or the momentum of the soul, not of flesh or romantic metaphor or the valentine shape with a piercing arrow carved on a tree. Some languages convey meaning well beyond the number of letters in its words. Arabic is one of these languages. A friend described it as more of the pronunciation of a symbol. It is intended to be a spiritually efficient way to communicate, one of depth beyond just speech and listening. It is conveyed through the feeling it elicits, which is why the listener is as accountable as the speaker, which is why the translations of such deeply mystic and beloved Arab and Persian poets require more than transliteration. It requires *qalb*.

Annihilation is salvation. The gift of truth is unwrapped from the inside. It ascends through the upwelling of love, an overwhelming disclosure, while our surface of bone and sinew disintegrates and descends. Death is the release of the incarcerated spirit, annihilation of the material container in which salvation awaits. It is, furthermore, the annihilation of distinctions and the unification of all beingness, everything subsumed into love as if there were never a parting between the multitudes, all One.

Some spend their lives recklessly tearing open a path to the heart when it beats softly through, patiently and joyfully awaiting the eroding from time. Annihilation is not the wanton destruction of the body but the soul's desire to return to the wholeness of its highest state. Dream, and take your time, lest your careless pursuits drift wildly from the path between your mind and your heart. Some truths you seek may be of no use in this lifetime, but rather in the timeless, unfathomable afterworld. Submit to the truth that seeks you.

Go There

When your attention is elsewhere,
you are called back.

You are never separate from your love.
It is separate from you.

Your heart is not inside you.
It is elsewhere, and you are inside it.

So where is your heart?
Go there.

Written

The Beloved
enters like a mist
when, in stillness,
it lays a kiss,
disarms my words,
and eludes my eyes.

On all empty pages,
the ink runs dry.
Hours gaze
from a clock sans face,
free from the hands
of time and space.

It's the pulsing chamber of light,
that of a lantern
of a wayfaring messenger who says,
"I am not writer; I am written."

An Empty Gift

A gift is fragrance out of breath
fled from the abode of the urn,
seeking respite of a wayfaring vessel
within whom it makes its return.

Be not daunted; open the cover.
Draw deeply from the spirit's fathomless well
Oh, water bearer for the soul of dry parchment,
a river of words erodes the truth a mountain can tell.

Lo, winds of wisdom for the seeking leaf
softly turns its empty pages.
Stir them not but deliver the stillness
spoken through the love of inner sages.

Leap not.
Be gently drawn,
dear sojourner, but not so soon.
Soft, the precipice waits for you to cast
from the abode of your own perfume.

Those who give, journey on
deep in the heart of those whom are given.
When the page seems dark, find the spark
as the flint of the lover strikes the Beloved's frizzen.

Where My Beloved Waits

Oh you pavement scuffers and ceiling crawlers,
why not upon walls of wheat and woodland over?
Jump the railcar, wayfarers.
What of floors of flower and dirt?
You're plodding through the pate
when you should be dancing through dharma,
reveling from the root.

There's a gypsy who never slumbers
even when she sleeps.
There's a field walker, a vagabond,
who fills his rusty tin cup with rasa
sprung from the fountain that flows in her dreams.
They drink an amber world and wipe flames
from their lips.

The wheat is razed to the soil line and below.
I've wandered into oblivion,
where my beloved waits.
Fanaa.
Fanaa.
Fanaa.

God, Truth, Love

The weary ghost insists that the conversation continue.
You're asking me for answers.
Being so conscientious, I'll do my best
to stay awake and talk, but it's gibberish.

I miss days of talking through an entire night into oblivion
until the sun lights a blue line across the horizon,
babbling until the air flees into zephyrs and we snap awake,
only to slumber the entire day in borrowed repose.

We humans were made to be commanded by our hearts.
This shell I haul around was a consequence,
a cloak with which to hide me among others.
True love is to remain hidden among the mysterious combustibles of
the heart.
Its sun fire leaps upward, casting light from the hearth of the eyes.
This is how we recognize love,
by the depth of deep of the hidden light and the length of the reaching
flames.

You say, "I like it when your consciousness is slipping away.
Your heart speaks, and it spins silk.
And only you can tie bows in the wildly flailing ribbons of flame!"
Leave it to God, the gift wrapper,
Who in turn leaves it to me to unwrap,
like a child with shortened breath.
We cannot desire the gift of truth long enough
before it comes to find us, bursting through the wrapping.

The great gnostics say, when we take one step toward God,
He takes ten toward us.
How am I to love a lover like that?
It's all within,
all within you.

Beauty outside comes from beauty within.
I'm not as bright as the moon, the closest we'll get to the true light,
but beneath its glow, I too am a reflector of the sun.
Sunlight is all white,
and the framework of atoms within the lattices of molecules
assemble and dance to bend such light into a spectrum of colors.

But there is a white light,
so pure which no prism can break into hues,
so white that ink flees the parchment of its pages.
Unable to describe with the mind of speech,
we are left with unuttered replicas
and then seek and love our journey through others
while not holding them idols.

God wakes us from sleep, but not from dreams.
Hold these illusions wordless in your heart.
Life is a touch, a kiss, the draw of a bow,
a bottom flagon of dreams overflowing the cup of reality.
I cannot touch the light that illuminates images.
Nor can I touch the images themselves,
only their matter.

We are shadows cast by light,
earth cast by breath into clay.
The moon is but a phantom without the sun,
a shadow of the earth.
All we have with which to love others
is what God leaves us.
You make it easy to speak
and do not hear my words as tricks of my mind,
making me awake but dreaming.

God is in everything, I do suppose.
O' Hafiz asks,
"Where shall I go from thy presence?
Thou art everywhere."

Love is a steady wind,
erasing what we know as soon as we try to grasp it.
It is pre-eternal wisdom,
named by God and whispered only to the heart.

The Elusive Garden

We pluck sweet and thorny words
like roses from the cacophony
and hand them to one another
in the vicissitudes of poetry.

From pre-eternity,
we are plucked from the garden of nonexistence
to dwell a while in the Garden of Imren.
We all are the wilting flower
in the elusive garden we seek.

In an Instant

Merciful pain reveals to you
that the ghosts of those you love
are real and those departed you thought were real
never were.

Do not unhand your own self-awareness
to take the hand of a divinely bestowed beloved,
for God takes back all His greatest gifts
except the one you give freely.

And you cannot give
what you do not yet understand.
You cannot be the wine
if you do not know your own intoxication.

Love withheld is an obstacle.
Love relinquished clears the path.
These two conditions,
like inhaling and exhaling,
are more important than breath itself.

Be what you become in this moment,
for each moment is a promised eternity
revealed within yourself
in an instant.

From Whence We Come: Morocco

It is the unsettled heart beneath the wool
fluttering the fabric over which we roam,
pulsing rhythms and melodies
that harken voices along paths unknown
to singing sands of harmony
recalling, recalling whence we come.

Content Sans Container

Words within wishes
have earthly limits,
but heaven's silent melody
hath no harmony on earth
but prayer and humility.

We maunder through time
in carriages of flesh and bone
with secret passengers
returning home.

By God's disclosure,
a parcel is unwrapped,
one last moment in one last gasp
as the aperture constricts
in the looking glass.

The spirit seeks refuge
long before the body dies,
gazing deeply into mystic abodes
otherwise hidden
from our human eyes.

Everything Is Becoming

We are left in the once-lost values of solitude and aloneness
that we might see
both the multitudes and singularity
in a single glance of paradoxical beauty.

Gibran says,
"Sadness is a wall between two gardens."
Perhaps it is one wall in one garden,
creating the illusion of two
and so preventing us from seeing
that they are *as both* One.

Sadness is a stark realization
that everything must run out.
Happiness is knowing
that this waning illusion of life
is the opener for all that persists
in the divine process
of *rebecoming* truth again.

The Key within a Key

We said we'd wake before the sun.
How many times had we done this before,
woken to silence with no words to speak,
no other beside us
to hear our plaintiff notes, fears, and wishes,
none but those that were lost to our minds,
waiting to be unleashed in a dreamer's visage.

Hungry thoughts pace the cage
of the consciousness, like a circus tiger
inches in front of you but miles away.
So it's you behind the bars,
unable to see it that way.

We woke
so we might find closeness
in freedom,
a companion waiting
poised in a moment as auspicious.

There, graceful in the waning night
and solitude before the soul of another,
it has only to create or fall back asleep.
Oh, to love purely like this,
through the bars between us
that others wrought.

And feel the hand of hope reaching in
past the sleeping guard of darkness.
It is how I am to release myself,
to release another,
for the key to her heart
is lost within my own.

Surrender releases the lock of an imprisoned heart.
Fear not what approaches;
relieve the guard.
What stirs this night is the green companion.
Here before has come again.
He takes the shape in a loving calm,
cup bearer, sweet wine, Dhul Jalal Wal Ikram.

Parched Earth, Quenched Heart

Beautiful mosaic
of a fragmented heart
is made of clay
and broke apart.

Parched by drought,
what more brings rain
to remembrance
than the Beloved's name?

In my silence
you hear how my burning thirst
mouths a drought of tears.

Hearts pump harder
when we bleed,
as absence sounds the hollows
of the waiting reed.

Into enormity of emptiness,
the vastness of the beloved to disclose
the sweetest water ever sipped
by the lover's parched and longing lip,
is the fragrance of the wine red rose.

What Is Not Reveals What Is

Who we are not erodes through time,
be it by water, wind, will, or wine,
gazing into the talus of our becoming
amidst the course,
drifts the fine.

Our purpose is to bear the breeze
with lips to cup 'til weakened knees
besotted within a life between
pre-eternal and post-eternity.

Thirsting through our body's gristle
flows the milk beneath the thistle,
you, true content sans container,
are pulsing spirit,
interstitial.

Clever Alchemist

I chanced to meet a ghostwriter at my door.
Her transportation failed just down the road,
a sojourning doppelgänger of sorts,
an elusive reflection in need of a tow.

Transmuting our words into wine,
we both sip time to time
until we collapse into catharsis
and rise again sublime.

Breathless with the afterglow
in the pulsing embers of a kiss,
our story wanes to a mountain of coal
for one last climb to the precipice.

And once at the summit,
we'll cast words adrift,
toast our glasses to flying,
and leap silently from the cliff.

I read your words by day
and skirt the wiles of your will,
but I know your heart by night.

Leave me, charlatan, to my waking hours.
I know whose ghost you are.
Why haunt my spirit in its sanctum by the light?
I contravene with tears
in the corners of your eyes.
Guide them back,
kiss their lids,
and send them off to hide.

In dark whispers,
calling you and calling you
to join them by their side,
why must you take me with you?
Is this protest not enough?
I importune to tender ears,
"I have things to do! I must!"

Still you pour yourself into my world,
an overflowing chalice,
and turn the wine to liquid gold,
oh, ever clever alchemist.

Die Beautifully: Empty Heart, Full Heart

Were a rose to know the gift of its own fragrance,
it would surely die fulfilled.

Sweet attar of its sigh
lulls open the red petals of my own empty heart.

Who could behold such hollowness
without imagining all it can hold when full.

'Tis recompense for the rose I draw in deeply
and die beautifully.

Niyat (Intention)

Inspiration is everywhere,
cast like beach sand flying off fleeing heels.
Still you have no idea where a single grain has flown.
It is not around you but within,
where there is not a where,
nor a thought that can be known.

Your *niyat* is like a pebble
dropped inside your shoe.
It can straighten the path of your itinerant soul
with nothing more to do
than bear a mild discomfort beneath your skin.
So then tell me,
without an intention,
wherever are you going, my friend?

***

Paying attention to the discomfort of a pebble in your shoe can cause you to wander astray. Endure the discomfort so that you might discover the results of your true intentions, your true direction.

Map to Your Heart

The map to your heart,
is in your heart.
So to get where you're going,
be still.

The guiding Light in mine
of which you seek
illuminates the path within yours.

Seek the One who points your soul
in love's direction.
He is pointing at you.

Ruined Life, Enlivened Death

Oh, Beloved,
since finding me,
you have ruined my life
and enlivened my death.

What more can one offer
in gratitude and remembrance?
This duality confounds me.
You are not my opposite;
nor I Yours.
The closest I can come
to being one with You
is to first be nothing.

How do I make work of this?
Unity lies in the infinite distance
of the great Artist's vanishing point.

I need only look to the farthest horizon
in this portrait of life,
where all lines in nature converge.
'Tis my end toward which
the beginnings of my foreground drift.

It Is

It is our silence He hears.
It is our thirst that drinks.
The heart pumps harder when we bleed.
It is the mass of absence
that moves the tides of company.
It is the vast emptiness
in which the enormity of the Beloved
discloses.

***

I find it interesting how we take the space we occupy for granted. For example, the couch in this room is contained within something (a space) whose primary characteristic is emptiness. And even that emptiness has a presence within something else. So does the couch somehow negate or displace space or do they coexist or collocate? In the couch's absence, nothing is there, but is the presence of nothing the same as emptiness?

Where in the *space-ness* of our constructed reasoning does emotion, thought, love, and bliss exist? In the absence of human consciousness or essence, nothing is there. Yet what is this notion of "there," and where is it?

In the absence of everything is nothing, which has no place and no time. This poem honors the nothingness through which everything in its latency flourishes on this earth and within our being. *Nothing* is *everything* waiting to become. How beneficent and permissive this *nothingness* is!

This Love Is Going to Kill Me

This love is going to kill me,
each remembered kiss a slice
to my heart,
drawing rivers of words,
to exsanguinate on pages upon pages
of never-ending ending.

Love bleeds like a sorrowful spring,
and yet I keep defending, defending.
Tonight is a night to embrace the lover
to rattle our shells from our ocean's echo
and stir like soul winds wound
in contrapposto.
An inhale cedes
in a sigh-sweet staccato.

Within the offset sheets of folded rose skin
cured as parchment,
there are pages to be opened.
A torch cast shadows on the heart's wall.
The rose is illuminated by,
and all are born from the light of creation.

Impregnated by dew,
a grape swells to a drop
to burst and roll down the green blade
of the vintner's sword into the goblet.

O tiny red ocean,
O fermentation,
release me now.
The ransom is paid.

He said, "I've plucked many roses
from countless bushes
and placed them in fine crystal vases.
But you are a garden
and I, to die,
have been placed within you
in placeless places."

This one catches flight on another's breeze
with so many crosswinds to the sea,
this one leather and that one caramel
to be brindle to be softened.
Kun faya koon.
Kun faya koon.
Be, so it is to be.
Oh, God, I hate this distance
that keeps my mouth watering,
watering for Thee.

Teaspoons of Light

I take in teaspoons of light
to feed the darkness,
and it still growls with hunger.

Nothing craves light
more than a shadow
with a secret it wants to show.

Sojourner

Across the surface, drag the hand
across knotted wood and obsidian.
Splinters sliver.
The skin is sliced through.
The surface bleeds an ocean blue.
Stroke the metal, torn and rusted,
pitted rock, and lichen-crusted.

Press the door, O sojourner.
Press the surface ever more.
Slide your fingers along the crypts,
a three thousand-year-old obelisk.

Reach through water.
Place a kiss.
The ears of God hears pious lips.
Leave your sandals on the step.
Enter this place as when you left.
Press the door,
its hinges hold,
behind the surface,
the secret's told.

A Cove One's Own

A cove one's own,
for hearts, a home
where sky and sea and
cliff sides crawling with posies
all meet in places
built from traces
of reassembled memories.

All is quiet.
All is tender,
purling waters to remember
sips to come from cups poured
by ocean waves en echelon
by providence and then beyond
by each embrace of pristine shore.
Reminding us,
O forgotten trust,
in things from hinterlands,
curves of thought imbued with love
raked into soft, hidden sands
washed away,
washed away
by the tide of the Beloved's hands.

Fractured Light

Even shadows choose to whirl
lithely in the beams,
romancing other silhouettes,
seeking revelation in their dreams.

Compassion, do not hasten them
nor wake them from repose,
for in the moment two dreams alight,
the awoken lover glows.

Stand boldly in love's mystery
as slings and arrows sail.
Through the strident journey.
hush, listen for the nightingale,
whose song seeps through a cloven heart,
mending fragments into one.

Seek the source that hides unbroken
in the brilliance of the Beloved's sun.

Recipient Becomes Sender

I'm just passing this gift along.
All has come to become gone,
but for a fleeting instant at most,
love is a guest of an eager host.

I become aware that sender I must be,
which is how it now arrives with thee.
This golden dove, thy gaze, our time
carried by messenger from the Divine.

This Bazaar, this cloud passing by,
is a trader's scale below a bartering sky.
'Tis only suspended by my arresting eye.
Then off again, I let it fly.

A poem, a song, a painful illness,
ecstatic whirling around the axis of stillness.
Gone from gone as gifts unwrap,
What's given is done to be given back.

Finding its way to hand and heart
by hand and heart that once had a start
as you who arrived had come before
I saw another close a door.

Waiting.
A package sent to ourselves
arrives like stars in a heart's black well.
I lean over the edge of introspection,
down to dark waters of a captive reflection.

On the ripples of light and shadow, I see
a present returned,
and the present is me.
Am I light emitted or light received?
Where am I on the wheel of destiny?
All I seek is its cycle's center,
blessed reunion of recipient and sender.

Why It Rains

My love expels from the aquifer of my being,
in synchrony with a mountaintop weathering.
Eroding rock is blown to dust,
coloring the sky red and rust.

Water gathers about the grain.
Then with its weight, it begins to rain.
Earth is quenched by pouring wine,
arousing the timeless out of time.

"Nothing is sacred,"
the sacred said
while drinking a drunken life
from the cup of the sober dead.

***

In its original version, the last couplet was written, "Pouring a drunken life into the cup of the sober dead." As I prepared for final printing, I changed this in honor of the "the sacred," an immensely enlightened friend who maintains esoteric relationships with those who've passed, either through the imbibing of their mystic poetry or in remembrance of their undying love. Drunk on self-annihilation and wisdom, we aspire to return to the eternal, a nonfleeting ecstasy of reunion with God. Once returned, what was once drunk on earth is now sober in heaven.

Paths Go By (adab)

I've taken to dubious endeavors
with the best intentions at stake,
far more receptive to the unknown possibilities
than the certitude of the choices
I'd otherwise make.

It's not always the easiest routes we find
among those of least resistance
with many a way to walk this path
and many a path to take this walk.
There's little heed for time and distance.

It's not about which road we choose,
as each shares a certain single end,
no matter how it dips and turns
or with whose a blessed journey blends.
No, 'tis not the path but how each step is taken.

Within the dark uncertainty,
a secret passage lies,
for we who keep our stirred hearts still.
From these shadows, truth will spill.
And to the surface, our purpose rises.

***

'Tis not the path, the steps taken. I am learning that there is a custom for behavior that, like a fine silk shroud, drapes across the nature of our true being, revealing its every curve, angle, and attitude. For me, *adab* is both the balance between what is the appearance and what is truth. The Arabic word Adab means to invite all or many people for all types of food, or a gathering around a table. Adab is etiquette and includes every noble characteristic, habit, or trait. Adab is a naturally developed trait and a state in essence that exceeds knowledge.

Where the Beloved Resides

How sorrowful to find ourselves
in the abyss,
lost across the seven continents,
seeking answers
when all along we are
amidst God's shoreless ocean,
surrounded by love.

Unseen, we run toward the truth,
but who alone can bear the pain
of a silent, solitary heart
that cries out to be relieved by company,
for it is there the Beloved resides.

I converted the single poem above into what is called a "2 by 2." Each of the two columns reads down as its own poem, or each row can be read straight across both columns. There are different meanings depending on the direction you choose to read.

Where the Beloved Resides (2 x 2)

How sorrowful to find ourselves	…	In the abyss,
lost across the seven continents,	…	seeking answers
when all along we are	…	amidst God's shoreless ocean,
surrounded by love.	…	unseen, we run toward the truth
But who alone can bear the pain	…	of a silent, solitary heart,
that cries out to be relieved by company?	…	for it is there the Beloved resides.

River Captain

I had no real idea what I was looking at,
as it seems a sublime visage foretells the future
and marks the past
more than it reveals the present moment.

Upstream and downstream
share the same unseen
source and destination both obscured.
They meet at the nexus of the boatman's consciousness.

There is one channel,
many rivers.
It's best not to confuse these routes
on our return to the ocean.

In-between-ities

There are immeasurably small instants
strung along an immeasurably immense eternity.
Beyond regret of moments once now gone
and those longed for to happen,
each moment is an in-between-ity.

This is the gracefulness of pure presence
when purely present.
Here at the node of infinity's lamniscate,
a unity so beyond you and I,
not even a we is fathomed.
Not here nor there.
Nor now and never.

Wisdom Beyond Logic

When the mind speaks,
wisdom puts a finger to its lips
and says, "Hush."

The fact I fail to find order in my life
is evidence that I am seeking the means with my mind
rather than the ends with my heart.

So I place myself in the path of wisdom
with faith that order finds me
before each next step is taken.

The mind is like the moon,
an illusion of beauty in the darkness of night
and an eclipsing silhouette arrested by day.

Wisdom is interrupted by the constant quest for order.
The mind is a thimble afloat in its vast ocean,
filling up with rain from the heavens,
riding low in the water
until it disappears in below the currents.

Signs

Why look for signs?
Why even expend an atom's effort to find them?
For we worry a mountain if we don't
and doubt when we do.

Nay, everything is everything,
and I have faith in the signs I don't see.
And the less I look with my eyes,
the more I believe with my heart.

Death and Life Share the Same Door

Whether abandoned by time or will,
the rose will endure past falling petals,
which reunite and enrich the soil,
from which it grows again.

Were I not to die and fall to earth,
of what use is this unnourished life?

A Fair Curve in a Slow Current

My death is a lengthening,
eastern shadow creeping
as the sun sets on a Westerner's life.
The fountain coins fall, deepening.

Throw away nothing
of a poet's reaping recollection,
glowing golden within the chaff,
darkened wheat in separation.

He plays to a spotlight,
an audience foreshortened
in the darkness beyond the true sound
of his winter-whitened curtain.
The azimuth of the eyes
reveals the sweetness
on his lips.

Their twisting of the rind
twirls a scent within the mist.
All is a poem in search of a song
and a song in search of a voice.

A fair curve in a slow current
need only *be*
without having to make a choice.

***

I wrote this over considerable time, but I completed it in a coffee shop in Boston the morning after watching my singer-songwriter friend, Chris Trapper, in concert. There was something about watching him on stage below the spotlights. I couldn't let it go.

Vast Encounters

How is it that such vast worldly encounters
can be taken in through such small portals
as our eyes and ears?

Perhaps the universe is already within us,
and it takes but a single ray of light
to illuminate its entire temple of the heart.

To behold the world like this
is to turn one's self inside out,
releasing a universe unto itself.

Let It Lie, Let It Fly

A feather softly landed.
Let it lie.
'Tis an attribute for yet another name,
an eternal light,
not intermittent flame.

When called through lips,
a sound becomes a kiss.
When a breath prays "love,"
it's lost to winds,
only to land
if it flies again.

Sated Fierce Ones

There is a sweetness when we realize
that all we seek on earth
is only for temporary nourishment
and that the truth flourishes among dreams
of the sated fierce ones.
What gives the lion his strength
is the softness of his dreams.

Bleeding Hearts

Hearts imbued with redolence
fill the garden with others sent
to pour their wine in the waiting chalice
of servants drunk in the sultan's palace.

Fragrance comes before the rose,
then long after the petals close.
Following the scent of flower white,
a nightingale came to rest one night.
Amongst the thorns she made her bed.
There from her chest, the colors bled.
So the red rose received its hue
from the winged messenger of Allah-hu.

Inspired Dusk

There is a moment before the sun sets,
just before the top of its crescent
disappears below the farthest
edge of the earth.
It is a divine promise of yet another
smoldering spectrum of marigold,
saffron, crimson,
and cobalt.
A promise of the day's last warmth
before night calls us
to dreams
before we smile,
knowing,
with the reminder on our skin,
that tomorrow the sun will come,
only to leave us with this pristine moment
once again.

Such splendid sweet endings are dawn,
never to melt into the same horizon,
never to burst with a less spectacular display
of heaven.
This is hope,
tumbling over and upon itself,
writhing like eddies,
lost in the directionless winds.

This amazement is just God,
sighing into the end of our day.

One and the Same, Respectively

In thought I stood in the hollow trunk
of an old and ailing willow tree.
I was filled with the wonder of its missing contents
'til the tree was filled with the wonder of me.

My blood and sinew,
bone and flesh,
never before this old soul met.
It wrapped itself around my heart,
which beat for us both as we both wept.

For without me, there'd be no we,
just two souls whose only purpose is to be
one who walks and one who waits
through life and death,
both consciously,
one and the same, respectively,
this hollow man and fulfilled tree.

Vertigo

Stored within us, beyond doors
we draw closed behind us,
year after year,
surrounded by loops and loops of locked
and rusting chains, is something
even more fundamental than faith,
an unabashed, boundless, and unbiased
openness.

We had moments in our infancy
through our early childhood,
where no one but God
was watching over us.

The chill we feel is a symptom
of the removal of shrouds that once
hid us from our inspiration
and still hides our preferred artistic medium
from us.

When you start feeling lighter again,
ascend.

The Baobab Tree

All are in repose
as a reddening sun sinks,
melodiously drowning
into a molten horizon.
My heart gasps in harmony.
Take me with you
before our time is gone.
I have not the strength to wait 'til dawn.

Long and low shadows of the baobab tree
yawn and crawl toward the east,
millenniums older than the father of Qasim,
tells us, "I have seen some things.
I have felt the slow passing
of many a wanderer,
each leaning upon me wearily."

Upended leviathans
with their dendritic branches
fly high in the Saharan azure
with barreled trunks plunging down and down
into the red soil of an aging earth.

Swollen bellied lions groan
and roll over in a heap,
exhaling the scent of steaming meat,
sweeter to them than the baobab fruit
that swings on vines from lofty roots.

Whiskers red and stained by blood
are tended by busying flies.
Claws retracted knead through dreams
of lions leading the prowling pride.

Sated and in repose, I watch.
The blood is still busy in my belly.
Dreams come without words,
sans ardent meanings
to fill the souls of predator beings
with a tranquil heart and absent mind,
free to drum with Gibran and Bayazid
to free the pulp of the soul from its bodily rind.

One Hundred Ways

A hundred ways
to remember the nameless
stand between the seeker
and that One never to forget.

Ninety-nine abandoned attributes
linger in the faint attar of imbued nostalgia,
wrenched in the twist
of the implacable ironwood.

The variegated visage of the Beloved
dissolves within distraction,
revealing the empty path of veracity
to maundering mendicants,
each collecting the dust of true essence
on the trailing skirts of their khirqas.

Lives bead and flow down a pillar of paraffin,
rendered free by the heat of a flame,
dancing wildly on the tip of a wick.
Lovers come undone
into river runs of melted awareness,
convening at the coast of consciousness,
surrendering to the sea
where seven continents of meaning marry.

Who Am I

I am the content
that has no container.

I am a sinner when I do right
and a saint when I do wrong.

I am the feeling that you're not alone
and the reminder that you are.

Of Those Arrived

For some,
the meaning of life is murmured over dinner plates
in silent torpor.
Its purpose is startled into realization
between clinking wine glasses.

For others,
it is to see deeply into our present
and to skirt the pulsing stars,
to find beauty in momentum
and embrace our presence
in the amber-lit windows
that frame the lives of those alight.

Wherever we are heading
is kindly guided by our certainty
of where we are now.

All We've Lost

Spin about a thread-fine axis,
collapse into a point,
and disappear into the universe
through the portal
of an infinitely small door.
Enter from always to never more.

Do this when you desire
that beyond earthly existence
and all you loved
within all that was lost
remains there in the realm
of nothingness.

Heart Becomes a Star

Heart becomes a blood-dense sun,
consuming all of anyone,
come to take a seat beside
or to sacrifice their burdens.

There goes the ghosts into the pyre,
softening,
silent from the ire,
consuming even their own ashes,
magnesium memories in the fire.

Until love fumes spheres of aural stars
humming distant in the cradling dark,
cuddled and lost,
yet guiding lights,
Hu remembers *where* you are
when *where* has forgotten
who you are.

***

We are to experience the universe from the center of the heart. Either deliberately or because I'm unable to articulate their distinction, the "heart" in this poem is intended to be One in God (Allah), for which "Hu" is the pronoun reserved only for reference to the divine. When we take our complaints or solitude to our heart, or if we beckon others to take company within ours, we summon the spirit (ghosts) of these beings to the all-consuming nature of a blessed heart. The essence of the heart resides in our center, yet despite its incredible power (potential), it becomes most mysterious and elusive when it comes to describing it, so I dwell on it here.

Magnesium burns extraordinarily hot and emits a blinding white light. It is said to originate in aging stars. Which themselves are of divine love. As a brilliant flame, it carries secrets to the universe and I'm using the reference to magnesium here, as a metaphor for the divine properties of the heart. Perhaps we are all entwined in the stuff made of stars. Our hearts are stars that guide others or are the beacons by which we are discovered and guided. The Sufi's refer to a "placeless place" and when we tie ourselves to places and times we often lose awareness of who we are. It is then that we can invoke the names of God to bring us back to that center of mystery.

Something is always as aware of us as we are aware of it. It is said that he who knows himself, knows God. Everything that comes into your heart while in your purest cognitive state is a reminder and a spark upon which to gaze and be consumed, ashes and all. The nothingness that is left and with which you are left is what the Sufi's might call the annihilation in God (fana). "Die before you die."

Inexplicable Certainty

The thought keeps cycling in my mind,
and I don't know why.
I've sensed less than this
of things I've known more.

The quiet, inward search for facts
fascinates me,
but even more so
that I cannot contain a smile
and nostalgic sense of happiness
inspired by the landscape
of this placeless place.

There are some mysteries in life
by which we are drawn out onto the precipice,
undaunted by where the edge might be
or whether we'll go over it.

And so I say,
I'd rather risk failure and sadness
navigating the playful patterns of my own uncertainty
than be happily swept away along the narrow path
of another's most certain illusion.

Somnol-essence

Hopes we take into our sleep
become the seeds of dreams to come,
fears then, the roots of nightmares.

Stir our hearts awake,
if you must.
Wind gypsies croon quixotic notes,
dappled like leopard in dandelion dust.

Caught in the clatter of castanets,
if poems were sheep, this one would be black.
That one is black,
and that one is black.

Pupils leap into pathos
without a splash.
That one is black,
and that one is black.

Somnolence is
when ripples lull
where all lambs go,
when somnolent,
when somnolent.

Signs to Fly

I dropped a palette of gold
that I pulled from the earth
to catch a single white feather
that fell toward me from the sky.

The gold was intended to pave the trail
from whence I came.
The feather was
to show me the direction I should go.

***

Two years after writing this, a feather literally fell from the sky in a
Caravanserai in Turkey. Since then, my entire life has shifted. This photo
is literally the moment I picked up that feather.

A Heart Filled with Emptiness

Everything enters my mind
through the hidden passages of my heart
on this journey of beauty.
wade not through details,
but whirl in wonder.

You complain of an empty heart,
yet drown in the rising tide of its echoes.
Your heart is not truly empty;
else love would most certainly have come to roost.

One that whines does not have an empty heart,
but rather a heart filled with emptiness.
Stop beating your fists against invisible walls.
You cannot push through a door that opens toward you.

You tie your turmoil into tiny silk satchels.
Steep them in bejeweled cups of boiling water
and stir bitter tea,
sweeten falsely,
drink up anxiously,
and burn your tongue.

Gather up the emptiness from your heart,
jump into the burning sun,
and bake.
Your emptiness is not sated by more content.
Those believing they hold a heart
have not the arms to let go.

When love finds you, do not receive it as replacement.
With whom but yourself do you barter, negotiate, and compromise?
Throw the merchants out of the bazaar.
All here is freely given
and received in the commerce of the heart.

Your beloved shining in your pellucid eyes
reveals the bounty within the shadows.
Dive deeper within those depths
filled with nothing but the awaiting.

Let rain fall in all directions.
Let water flow upstream.
Be all that you are not
and let not what you are
become all that you wish to know.

Real Love in a Series of Affirmations

- Real love is the endlessness of a mirror's own reflection.

- Real love binds the sheep, the wolf, and the shepherd together in passion.

- Real love is an impenetrable wall between you and what you think you love.

- Real love cannot be given by or to nor forged into a palace soaring around us. It is only submitted to within the fathomless self.

- Real love is more patient with us than we are with it.

- Real love is lost in the beginning of a whisper and returns at its end, screaming.

- Real love is jealous of any other kind of love.

- Real love can have warm lips in the winter and a cold heart in the spring.

- Real love is the last that you will learn of yourself when you first know it within another.

- Real love is just beyond where the tip of the flame disappears.

- Real love is shared between constants, not variables.

- Real love is as it should be, not as it is.

- Real love is brilliant flash giving us but a glimmer of our frailty.

- Real love is the very same mortar between the bricks of the mosque, the church, and the synagogue.

- Real love persists most when it is pursued least and never fled.

- Real love is in the direction a broken compass points.

- Real love is the last ticket to anywhere, the water, the ferryboat, the captain, and, most of all, the continents it spans.

- Real love leaves no trace of it ever having come; its footprints are yours.

- If you find real love, let go of it. Do not name it. The real Real will find you.

Chapter 3

Poems with Rounded Edges

Introduction

"Poems with Rounded Edges" is intended to be softer sounding poems, nostalgic reflections, self-portraits of a writer, and other general reflections on human conditions such as friendship and youth. If you are reading chapters in numerical order, this one provides some relief in intensity, hence softer "rounded edges."

Nostalgia is an intoxicant to most writers and poets. The poems in this chapter are looking-back reflections on life gone by and looking-in musings of lives unraveling. What triggers nostalgia has always amazed and baffled me. How is that nocturnal sounds, natural lighting at dusk, or a sucker punch to the heart sends us spiraling back through the passage of time?

I hope that these poems inspire you to take stock in how you see yourself in the world and that you embrace the narrator of your own life and prepare to be marveled, lost, exalted, betrayed, and reminded.

If we attempt to internally verbalize our feelings, many of us are drawn to metaphors. And really, what more is a word than a mere approximation of its intended meaning? These poems tend to revel in metaphors, that is, to find big, bold, beautiful words. For such is poetry.

Some may sing meaning to you versus dictate. In fact, in this and the next chapter, you may find the poems are better read aloud as one would do in spoken word or slam poetry.

As we discussed this chapter, my dear friend wrote,

"As I read, the signposts that glared out along Skip's journey are very similar to those along road I have travelled and so it is easy to be co-travelers. And as it happens amongst co-travelers, one points out to random things along the path; jumping from a tree on the sideway, a stone sticking out of the ground, the interruption of a hurrying squirrel, taking in the melting sunset, or absorbing the quiet and listening to what it has to say. Conversations among us co-travelers are often incoherent, and it would be hard for many to and a thread between them, yet both intuit that the thread is the road. The haphazard references, woven into this chapter, thus become our souvenirs and hold value for us. These meager souvenirs take on a bigger meaning and a deeper significance. For me personally, as an artist, they provide hope and inspiration. And from an artistic perspective, they accomplish their biggest goal at the outset ... so everything else the reader gains from her reading, is a bonus." (Arshia Qassim)[8].

---

[8] Arshia Qassim, Letters to the Author, March 2015

Some Friends Are Like the Leaves in Fall

Some friends are like the leaves in fall.
From the verdant spring, they unfurl
in their splendor and vibrancy.
In soft whispers and summer hiss,
they stage the hues of blossoms and ballads
and whistle birdsongs from hidden branches.

Elevating from their ecstatic state of equinox,
these satellites drift into the so longs of solstice
and from hue to hubris, calling "come hither."
Lofty leaves dance, whirl, and vault
in the autumn air for new friends of fair,
who too will turn like bookish pages into pulp.

Fly from twig in twilight!
Oh, friends,
fade to saffron, russet, rust,
and carmine to cobalt into forgotten pyres of time.
Fall friends,
fall into the dirt and dust,
for in the spring your soil shall route the roots
from which fresh leaves feed, unfold, and revel sublime.

Blood Moon

Istanbul, 2013

A blood moon arrives
on the last trace of a new fragranced wind,
that of withered petals and peat,
curling bark, and spilled leaf pigments.

It is a steady procession
from the respire
of summer-weary tree roots
to the pale, trembling banners
of their limbs in distress.
Against the rouge sphere waves
these restless silhouettes.
It whirrs
behind the sound of crisp chips
scuffing across concrete
and nondistinct exclamations
wrestled from the foliage.

Our minds wander far off in the fall.
We break free
into states of disassociation with
present memories,
and we

recommence our thoughtful audit
of the past and moments yet to happen.

Pray we are rescued by our hearts
as the season's sinking deepens
before the blood
runs
dry.

This photo was taken by the author with a handheld camera in Istanbul, 2013. I couldn't stop looking at her.

My Highway's Washed Away

Sitting at my desk,
crisscross applesauce,
I gasp like a dying child,
dying to flee the corpse of a man.

I, not a child anymore,
whose imagination is a broad highway,
layered between the wings
of a dragonfly.

Behind me,
stumbling the furrows,
dust from age trails in the eddies.
It is I, running like a child.

Wagon wheels gargle and giggle
ungreased, unglued.
Another child watches and watches,
fingering ninety-nine pebbles in her pocket.

Dandelions blink awake
from dust sown.
Sun-pinched wishes
lost lashes behind me.

We, not children,
chase circles into soil,
tightening the noose
around the son of the father.

Dragonflies sip morning reflections
from a smooth surface pond.
Here, my highway's washed away,
and all before me and all behind,
is gone, gone, gone.

Child's Prayer

Love reigns and quenches;
it gives warmth as it shines.
It dances among us,
holding hands across time.
Like rain over mountains,
its tears wash them down
across fans of alluvium
and then carving the ground.

It pours into rivers,
knitting braids over sands,
like confluent families with interlocked hands
that lift you up high so you may see
that I'll love you from God,
over mountains and seas.

I'll not cloud your thoughts with trite explanations
but offer my heart for illumination
of bright shiny engines that gleam along tracks
through dark nights and tunnels,
there again back
to a home that glows in you,
wherever you are,
like the navigational light of a boat captain's star
that guides like a chorus,
for all who'll hear it
from angel to prophet to your heart's inner spirit.

From He who will bless you with the love for another,
what He weaves together, nothing renders asunder.
For love endures life, its frailties, and trials
as each of us cries or breaks into smiles.

You roam in my prayers,
held close little one,
and a house has a door,
but a home has none.
So for now, let me hug you,
and whisper a prayer
that you can keep with you,

even if I'm not there.
"May God smile upon me;
keep my family in sight.
Teach me forgiveness.
Guide our days and our nights.
Protect me, bring comfort.
And Lord, I thank thee
for the blessing of love,
bestowed upon me."

Boat Called Rock Bottom

Why would anyone set sail
on a boat named
Rock Bottom,
yet here I am.

The sky winked a few times.
The day spilled slowly and steadily
out over the horizon.

Millions of people cursed it, loved it,
or wished it had never come.
But with no heed to us,
the day crossed the finish line,
tired and worn,
collapsing into the arms of dusk.

Winding to a Point

A child stooped low and picked up a stone
about yay big with a rounded edge.
He could find no reason to put it in his pocket,
so he jumped to his feet instead.

The boy's eyes narrowed as he thought of this stone
about yay big with a soft, smooth face.
He could find no reason to keep it in his hand,
so he drew back his arm and aimed.

His thumb and forefinger curled around the stone
about yay big and obsidian black.
He could find no reason to wait any longer,
and his arm sprung like a steel trap.

The youth caught his balance as on went the stone
about yay big with a glistening sheen.
It skipped once … twice and lost its momentum,
disappearing in the ripples of the stream.

So are the thoughts of aging men
holding dreams in the palms of their hands.
They cast their stones along the surface of time
and spend their lives trying to find them again.

***

This poem takes the reader across a man's lifetime through specifically chosen words in each stanza. It moves from a child to a boy and from a youth to a man. And with each stanza, the same stone being thrown changes in its appearance. Always beautiful and mysterious, it changes from rounded to smooth to obsidian black to glistening and then to aging, and poignantly it is always thrown away.

Think of the important things you've thrown away or let go: notebooks, memories, lovers, and friends. Are we really letting them go? Or perhaps we are experiencing a loss of appreciation for what we persistently have within us, like a cat running from its tail in box.

The release of something shares an intricate relationship with what we seek. How will we ever find that which we already have? This wantonness is understandable as a child, but at some point, we must mature to realize that we are constantly seeking the same thing, disembodied love. You can throw away the person, but not his or her meaning. And so, that which we throw away always draws us back, and we seek them again.

The Empty Heart of the Poet

Only poems that reach toward such heights
send their roots so deep into sorrow.
Tears of gold fill the cups that we hold.
And the drunker we get,
the more sober by morrow.

But if you search in the shadows of an empty heart,
more worthy you are when it's time to depart,
for there alone in the prospering dark
is the light of Love to be given,
not borrowed.

Composition in Completion

I was once the music of my era,
so melodic and lyrically astute,
and I painted myself
into the foreground of a song
and became both composer and instrument.

I've become the narrator of my own drama—
the protagonist, villain, and victim—
the watering pair of candlelit eyes
waiting in the wings of life
for my denouement to begin.

You are the soft curves
of a smile that cradles remembrance,
pooling in the palms of prayerful hands,
harmonizing with the Sahara's singing sands,
all of nature in peaceful cadence.

Music is the bell of nostalgia,
ringing softly in the distance.
I follow its calling,
as a bee who seeks
the saccharine path of reminiscence.

'Tis in our nature to stop and sip
from the sweetest pool of time gone by
and then, once quenched, open our wings
into the sibilant breeze of destiny
and live a ballad while we die.

Gray Good-byes

Morning stirs a dull gray mist,
clouding memories of your tender kiss.
And where angels once leapt upon my heart,
there's only wreckage as the storm departs.

I remember when we laughed in sighs
and walked through the sands under seaside skies,
kicking up fragments of mother-of-pearl
and paving roads of color into another world.

And where stars blink on,
as I close my eyes,
waves curl over,
and a heron flies
where the coast goes dark
from a crimson sky.
It's there my cobalt blue
turns to gray good-byes.

There's thunder in our hearts,
and they beats in time.
And when you breathed out a promise, I would breathe in mine,
but while the angels played music on fragile strings,
you lost my voice in the lines that another sings.

You were there beside me when I was alone,
but it wasn't really me that you were waiting on,
and we kept paying love, no matter what the cost.
But love can't return the time that we'd lost.

And where stars blink on,
as I close my eyes,
waves curl over,
and a heron flies
where the coast goes dark
from a crimson sky.
It's there that cobalt blue
turns to gray good-byes.

There are oceans and mountains that I've yet to cross,
and a sun might rise and melt this painful frost.
But somewhere in the distance of this cold, dark night
is a last angel singing to my guiding light.

And where stars blink on,
as I close my eyes,
waves curl over,
and a heron flies
where the coast goes dark
from a crimson sky.
It's there my cobalt blue
turns to gray good-byes.

(a song)

Timeless Through the Ages

What is timeless through the ages
is conveyed in the pages,
etched in stone or vinyl.
And what has a beginning
will reach many ends,
but none is ever final.

The hope you seek
in the words I speak
is far deeper than their meaning can reach.
The paradox is
that hope doesn't serve a future
as much as it does the present.

Abandon sight of its sign
and have faith that it is here.
"What of me next?"
we ask of our sages.
"Will I thin to a point
and be lost in the vagueness?"

All of our choices
as we sort through
those pained and conflicted voices
succinctly describe ambiguity.
Hold on to anything but time.
Hold on to your words,
and let go of mine.

Waiting to Be Picked

Trays of drinks fly by on the Texas breeze,
delivered by waiters with wings on their heels,
carrying courage to the sober in dire need,
those who will never read my poems,
those hard hearts and parched throats tough as steel.

I was the last one picked for the kickball team.
Me and the other kids fought the hurt, staying strong,
waiting to be seen by our idols,
not caring what side we'd be on.

And here at this table, I ask,
"How did I land in this roadhouse cantina,
moving to the same old emotional dance,
the same old childhood song?"

My billed cap is pulled down over my brow,
as I prefer to not be noticed in the din of this drunken schoolyard.
How magnificent a God that hears each and every call
of billions and billions of the last waiting souls,
each picked first by the captain of his very own heart.

So Jung and So Sang Freud

Quietly sighs the dawn,
long and languid through the hours.
All to come about lies in wait,
per chance to say
something sagacious,
something great.

Dreamers are wide awake,
so erudite and perspicuous,
as if their dreaming
were to dream
away the smothering incubus
that sponges up the will to act
by a forlorn soul expecting
that fortune's grin will have its heart
as effortlessly as its wanting.

Stock-still and stunned of mobility,
tipped teaspoons heaped with emptiness
spill into steaming cups of void,
sipped by thirsty lips of the *young*
on the blarney stone,
a kiss and tongue
to speak their yearning with *sang-froid*.

I Polish Mirrors

My story is the collision of what I say
with what you hear or
something careless.
That is what I'm here for,
just a sentence
poorly wrapped,
a bow untied,
unzipped,
unstacked.

All fallen rose petals
underwatered
wilted pages
Roots of wounded
Periphrasis
Antlers shed
Their velvet read
with some words flown
from lips and bone.
So much is left unsaid

Forensics show my story stumbled.
Witnesses heard three shots fired.
My story bleeds channels
along sidewalk seams.
It seems my time's expired.

The fact I was right-handed
makes my writing
average,
marginalized.
A ricochet of plans went awry.
Life stays two paces
ahead of mine.

Still this story missed its stop,
and now it's back to the pages of *your* story again.
When do I drop my polishing cloth?
Where does this sentence end?

Life Is the Dancer

Life lies in state beneath my fingertips,
held at bay by the stay of my hand,
poised in the breeze
as the weight on the keys
starts to tap out the song of a man
that sparks a light in this torpid gray matter,
stirring an earthbound chance for
my soul to repose
and my pen to compose
a dance for life as itself, the dancer.

A Juxtaposition of Self

I never questioned the prognosis of my own gallantry
until taught the word *bravery*.

I knew nothing about success
until I experienced failure.

I never feared death
until I overlooked living.

And I never knew a friend
until I was called one.

The Writing Hand Is Raised a Slave

"Such tiny hands," he said,
shoving elephantine thoughts
into them,
wielding such power,
knife-clutching,
pen-caressing.

He took his eyes off the screen
for a moment
to watch them go.
He pondered,
"Long is the journey along nerves
from heart to paper.
Nothing can be squandered."

One day his hands will die,
having bled for God and country,
having spit and wept
along the path,
tapping time
from the tip of his fingered infancy
to the top of his wrist,
where youth dons a hero's cloak,
stirring loins in angst,
fire carriers of thrumming tribes
whose eyes purl water
from the smoke.

Then up arm and shoulder
shuffles age,
a road along his neck
that forks
where one goes south,
where memories start.
The other heads toward the forgotten north.

Fateful, the besieged tellurian
seeks whence his end began,
a northern throne for
a southern heart,
who thereupon ascends and proclaims,
"I've come to free this writing hand."

Putting the Tea to Boil

I'm putting the tea to boil,
finding a spot on the earth in which to sink
a heart string to play,
my mind to think and untangle a knot of toil.

I'm putting the tea to boil,
something warm to come.
Porcelain cups and waiting lips,
hibiscus leaves and red rose hips
within the heart a thrum,
stirs a ripple in a steeping conundrum.

My last verse has gone missing.
Its sound, sans words, lost in half-slumber
so half-awake and torn asunder
by answers hissing and then bristling.
Then comes the awaited harmony of a kettle whistling.

Humans

Wherever they are gathered,
they are sure to draw attention to themselves.
They are unable to avoid the same eventual malady,
but their symptoms are beautiful to behold.
They are painters of great landscapes,
yet challenge painters to capture their colors.
Their greatest moments come during their downfall.
And our rejuvenation comes with their rebirth.
They are the harbingers of memories
of when we climbed among them.
Yet they harbor children in their earthy smell and dampness
before they return again to the earth from the pyre.
They are from various branches of the same order
and keep their life force locked in large cells,
which escapes as the year wears on,
eventually killing the jailers
and battering down their homes.

But were they not to die,
they might never be born.
Were they not to mingle in the eddying winds,
they would remain quite content,
but all the less noticed.

Regardless, wherever they are gathered,
they are sure to draw attention to themselves.
Humans, be humble, lest we forget
the wonder of tree leaves.

What We Do, We Are

Often we stand on the fallow banks,
transfixed before such a sullen river.
Some remain fixated with a distant vision
of the opposite shore.
Others see just the abysmal current
that sequesters them, slumbering by.
And then there are those with imaginations
drawn to action,
who cannot help but see a bridge.

Wordness

I read.
I listened.
I composed
what might resemble a word.

And then I realized
that the innermost attribute of a word
is wordless
wrapped in word-ness.

All I could think to say
is all I could feel in silence,
just
I … I … I.

A Seed Found Furrow in My Brow

A seed found furrow in my brow
awaiting harvest, hungers now.
Through my fertile mind's palimpsest,
a vine breaks soil where memories nest,
pushing on with a writhing stem
from deep brown earth toward blue welkin.

With nostalgic rays, a star unfolds,
a leaf, a story yet untold.
Each bud is a poem that's yet to bloom
in flowered couplets for the moon,
awaiting dawn,
for petals pleat
to release a blossom's fragrance sweet.

And from one strand, a spider weaves
a gossamer web on trembling leaves
to capture prey that seeks to read
poetic verse among the weeds.

Plant and spider thus conspire,
conscripting minds of like, inspired
to sew words of thorns that never wilt
'til every bough a bookshelf built.

(this poem is a collaboration with friend and author, Maureen Seaberg)

The Noisy Ones

With little heed to the sanctity of silence,
morning is maddened.
Everything howls and screeches,
barking on queue.

Little fish flip themselves
up through the surface,
seeking water striders,
unaware bees wings buzz tiny vortexes.

Cows moan across the lake
in the hidden woods,
fat on the grain
from which they'll be slaughtered.

Beyond the sun-turned lilies,
crows pause to decipher the mockingbird,
but the message is unclear,
so it's back to their murder and mayhem.

I have vertigo out on the pitted dock,
staring down at rose cloud reflections
fallen from the sky,
brush stroked against the tidal currents.

A light winds ripple crosswise
in all this cacophony,
and nature tells me that
I am the noisy one.

This Moment

This moment shall never be forgotten,
here and now, the first in the endless sequence of
breathless pirouettes that lie before us
like promised sunsets fulfilled.

This moment will never be forgotten,
the last in the progression of a gently walked trail
dappled with the pattern of footprints, some solitary.

This moment will never be forgotten,
like the link in a chain that tethers our past to the unfolding future.
It is the capstone of continuity, a harbinger of perpetuity.

Of all grand moments that I will ever remember
are those that are always next
that wait like the new woken eyes
of dreaming foxes.

I Remember a Time When I Didn't Have to Remember

I remember a time
when I didn't have to remember a time,
when butter only came in sticks, not tubs,
when the trash men came every morning,
when a Chevy was just a Chevy (and my dad parked it on the street
for free),
and when the cops would give us kids warnings.

I have memories of
when freedom smelled like barbecue sauce and Kingsford coals
and my fingers tasted like Old Bay.
We crunched corn on the cob
and sat with lit faces beneath fireworks,
not waiting and watching from our cars, miles away.

I remember when
it wasn't who had the bigger yard,
but which yards could be conjoined to make
the biggest football field
and our parents' voices,
not cell phones,
called us to gather around the supper table.

I remember when
lawyers were great
because we hardly ever needed them,
when we feared dying more than being poor
when we called them jobs,
not income,
back then.

I remember when
an endless ringing phone
or even a haunting busy tone
required no further investigation
because at least you knew
she was home.

I remember
when love meant you didn't have to stop looking.
"Just keep looking at me."
Romantic love didn't grow in diversions
like weeds in fertile soils of commiseration.
I remember you looking at me.

I remember
when you could hear me draw a tranquil breath
between each spoken rhyme
rather than me listening alone
to memories tapped
into liquid crystal diode lines.

Destiny Stifles a Question

Fate brings people of purpose together
in places, at times, under auspicious conditions,
and I am amazed and treasure the cluster of humans
when I consider the origin of these encounters.

And still we question and consider too much
in search of wisdom's inventions
where I beseech destiny for answers
while destiny beseeches me
to stop asking questions.

Ode to a Roadrunner

Diamond-hard headache,
you have a chemical in your left hand,
and the door outside is to your right.
Take the pavement quickly.

Oh, wrinkled earth,
do you feel my gentle journeys
across your skin?
I am the unfaithful sojourner
whose paths deepen the creases of grief
that guide your tears toward the ocean.

Lamenting earth,
do you quake for the dead I've buried
a few feet beneath your surface
or choke on your own blowing ashes?
Have I been the cause of your tears
that fill the ocean with salt?

I traverse your land afloat on rivers of fear
in search of a sea of fulfillment,
while others bravely sail your oceans of doubt,
seeking the firmness of dry land.

I'd searched for a remedy
until the search itself became my malady.
I'm dying and nearly six feet deep into your skin,
replaying life in the width of a road crack.
Above me, rain puddles freeze and thaw,
freeze and thaw.

I found love in the Philippines,
laughed with Slavic sailors,
and drank with Swedish shipbuilders
in the Port of Inchon.
I became homesick on Rottnest Island.
I felt the tempest of history
on an early morning train to Heidelberg.
I climbed into your caves in Cappadocia,
and I saw formations of women in burkas
doing Zumba along the Persian Gulf.

I cried into the clouds for him on a mountain.
I swallowed my soul mate whole in a caravanserai
and was consumed by her from the inside.
I forgave my dead father
within the flames around a campfire.
I thought to write this in my mind
here during my road running.

I'm amazed at how vast and hollow I am,
filled with nothing.
The universe follows me,
ticking on my wrist.
My time is up.

Tear Streams in Renditional Evolutions

In this moment, eyes fill with tears
from a voice,
a song, once filled our ears.

Today could quench an aching world back then
if we'd just all fall in love again.

O gather up those endured sorrows,
my lovely friends of yesteryear and morrow.

And set sail on these saline streams
toward *remember whens* foretold in dreams.

There, time and distance have no say.
There, we arrive again to ne'er again part ways,
and what was once is happily, magically,
then and now for always.

Two Red Rockers

Encouraged by promises I made to myself,
I am chased by memories of dreams that never come true.
Here in the maundering dereliction of presence
are coffee brown moments in blue.

Stones unturned;
life kept at bay,
swept back by aromas and flavors
of a distant past beckoning anew,
awoken by the rattling of discontent sabers.

Tears in the Thirsting Years

How intriguing to fathom the labors of love,
staring up from a fathomless well,
as if happiness might lift the wings of a dove,
clipped and weeping in the hollows of hell.

With great stealth, it navigates the depths of doubt
to overtake a torrent of tears,
a deluge of hope to quench the drought,
precious seconds to the thirsting years.

Time-Bitten Memories

Rhododendron and fresh mown zoysia grass
Fragrant halos that come undone
Fumes of creosote oozing from poles
Sweating tar under a scorching sun.

Sap on sodden pine needles
glow wistfully like amber tears
that fall through vaporous piles of leaves,
decaying beneath layers of years.

Oil-stained sand behind a gas station
Dew-soaked chat on the tracks,
draining colors of autumnal dusk
into after-bedtime black.

Solar apparitions in purling glass
diffuse through Venetian curtains.
Star chip white bespeckles the night,
where no warmth of color is certain.

Splinters of hope and anguish
peel like paint off the ironwood transom
of my family's boat, set low in the water,
while our spirits hold fast to the stanchions.

Our mother's love playfully chases us
through the biting measures of time.
Silhouettes run and ripple down rows
of linen memories that dry on the line.

Rain Interrupted

The sun pranced out after
the curtains of rain withdrew,
as if it were some radiant hero,
as if we weren't humbled by anonymity,
pleasant, numbing, insulating
from such villainous precipitation.

Maxfield Parrish sighs.
"The artist is always too late to his easel."
Missing the sheets and shards,
the splash and writhing hiss
of small united raindrops
terminate on the ground
in a death pact.
Shhh, martyrs of bliss.

I wish the showers to stay
to drown the sun just once.
Aspirating glaucous, somber, gunmetal gray,
most perfect lines speed vertically down
through a windless,
most-unhoped-for day.

Chased by the lumbering sledge of Thor
hastened by this ancient molten core,
it is drawn down by gravity
once more.

I slide shut a thin glass door
for the villain and hero to rumble on.
Rumble on.
The spoils poured upon the victor.

Don Quixote

For Alonso, the day was sinking into dusk.
But for Dulcinea, her knight was rising.
Long his lance's shadow stretched,
just like his stories, picaresque.

He flaunts his tale of espionage,
purring silent and clandestine
"There I sprung from camouflage," he exclaims,
"and smote these vile leviathans!"

"Oh, please don't stop," the gypsy cries,
draining doubt from starlit eyes
from behind her fan of elegant slips.
She retracts the rivets to her lips and sighs.

Alonso mounts the moment of his concupiscence
to rescue the fair Dulcinea from her diffidence.
But the windmills turn for our quixotic man
whose delusions are rescued by a chaste heroine.

Years later, a man was overheard in Cordoba,
el estaba hablando con unas senoras
"Oye musas, puedo decirte,
he visto algunas cosas."

"Mi vida se salvo una noche estrellada
por una mujer de gran belleza
que volvio a las tablas de la fortuna
aqui, en mi reino de Iberica."

Chapter 4

Poems with Sharper Edges

Introduction

"Poems with Sharper Edges" contains poems that were mostly written rapidly under unusual or auspicious circumstances or within austere writing environments (or both). I might have just seen an act of mercy or one of extreme cruelty, or I saw an athlete in the news caught using steroids, or someone pushing around all their belongings in a grocery cart who said Merry Christmas to me, or maybe I remembered the betrayal of an old friend or a soured romance. These are all actual or remembered moments of personal transformation. Each moment at any time could become a future stimulus that might change my view of the world or its view of me.

As I observe the world around me—whether across a coffee shop or over continents oceans away—I reflect on its events from such varying perspectives whether they be sarcasm or mischief in mind, frustration, self-loathing, disgust with the world's darkness, boredom, or simple playfulness. Some of the poems flirt with our wild and raw side, the ego, and those parts of us that we might be afraid to show to even ourselves.

I try to write unabashedly, only to realize that what is even more difficult than writing what is on my mind is *not* writing what is on my mind! One's mind can be a confusing place to others and it takes a good deal of restraint or control to keep it hidden or disclose it in all its glory. As I evaluated which poems to include in this chapter, I admit that I have withheld my edgier poems, which itself is a bittersweet illustration of how we are often unable to let our minds go anywhere beyond the paper on which they are written (if we even get that far). We put up our own roadblocks, dear friends. We complain about imposed censorship in society, but censure our own minds. We marvel at the nonconformists who have shaped the world of art, business, or politics, and yet we see them as ideals to which we must conform. All this being said, I also respect a balance of etiquette and civility when we communicate.

I hear the profane and absurd all around me and watch so many wrestle with perspectives on life through their sharp words. I'm not immune to this wailing. How can one be when this world throws everyone and everything at us with such velocity and volume? I find resistance more dangerous than submitting to awareness. Besides my filters are not always intricate enough to sift the wheat from the chaff before it becomes an important ingredient for the recipe of thought. So as it is with anything you read, do so at your own risk and do not be quick to judge the writer for his words, for his heart ricochets the bitterness and abhorrent, which also makes up life's flow.

Ten-Pound Poem on an Ounce of Paper

Harvesting thoughts,
with a scythe and sickle,
filling in the furrows
like a paradox popsicle.

The literary farmer
sows fertile periphrasis,
lamenting fraught seedlings,
twisting taffy from the pages.

While carmine dust devils
stir the desert air,
cochineal insects
sip on prickly pear.

Gather and dry,
and then pulverize
into bittersweet colors
of pomegranate dyes.

Waiting for the Mulch to Arrive

On Saturday morning, waiting
for the mulch to arrive,
a particular pattern of a bird
chirps,
and as I compose
the chantey,
water striders stand still
on a winter fountain's parting tear.
Espresso, cupped,
buttered oak steams
flavored expressions,
become this moment's poem before
a day of poetry
appears.

Glowering Junkies

A glowering beat junkie
shuffles frayed hems over the avenue.
I am propped up and preened.
Through the door he trips
to find a pew.
All this, I watch with a dour view.

Down in a beanery
where souls are served
coffee with a shot of consciousness,
who nibble on curated cakes of turd,
awaiting liberation from these surroundings.
It's a cacophony of diatribe, cackles,
and disenfranchised, dim-witted opining.
Counting,
in quarter time of a song I'd sing to myself
if this woman before me would just
stop talking
over the music in my headphones.

She's speaking to me from a bag of bones.
"You resemble my brother at Microsoft."
I asked, "Well, is that good?"
And then she asks if I too work at Microsoft.
I detach one earplug and imagine spitting at her feet,
replying, "I can't imagine why I would."
Crazy.

We dare to thrive
like dew clung to a thin thread of spider silk
and how we slide
down in a moment, a little more
when the breeze of our prey
quivers the chord.

My deeper thoughts ride out
on the tip of a swordfish
dipped in fine-finned fears
from the undercurrents of this vicious tide
to throttle the banshee that screams with eyes
filled with crystal tears
that fall into my coffee mug
and sweeten the slake
of our bitter drug.

Men Entering Women

He tried to tie her to the bed with the clothing
wrangled off during her writhing.
But it was he who was ensnared by her flesh.

She laughed at him
as he became impotent during the battle.

It seems a man will wear himself out
trying to enter the realm of a woman when he is
unable to see the real door to her heart,
no matter how naked they get.

Todays "Best Sell By" Date

These days the "sell by" date
dictates the menu for my morning meal.
The next torpedo through the torpor
will be the sound of last night's unfinished dinner
scraped into the centrifuge of my garbage disposal,
separating hardened gruel into graduated densities
of curiosity.

The absinthe must have done our cooking
as I'm not familiar with the remains
and I can't even boil water.

Damning the torpedoes,
I ponder my death
and my whirring mind
as it spins apart the densities of a girl
still passed out in the crevices of my couch,
spun-out shards of cold, pungent pulp.

I need something for the pain.
Instructions on the label read,
"Take two pills on an empty soul, and
call your publisher in the morning."

Writing on an empty stomach
only exacerbates this unfulfilled addiction.
My motivation is a hope that one day
I'll overdose on literary completion
and die quietly in the dawn
beside my "best used by" date.

Kissing Andromeda

There is a fat, mad woman.
Her head pokes through burlap.
Andromeda's prodigy is in my space,
poking me with her ballpoint pen.
Her lips are flapping and smacking spittle.
Waxy smears appear on her chin,
a protruding peach pit knob.
Drained and unkissed lips
wrapped tight over warm pink gums.

Too late, she sees me.
Abandoned by gravity,
lost focus in her black melton,
she pauses, closes her eyes,
and, with sighs, breathes me
into a hail of dislodged teeth,
spewing dust tails
like cold, crazy comets.

Andromeda sways and lurches.
Our tongues touch and flicker,
while I'm mouthing
deeply muted thoughts of madness.

Story of You

Auto-writing on the Train

The story of you is mentioned in
a polished mirror.
My story is the collision of what I say and what you hear.
My expanding waistline is filled with regrets
and fallen rose petals.
I am just words poorly wrapped
with a brain as a bow.
It falls off
as my story smears behind me
in blood stains from open wounds
from many of life's steel shaft arrows
and ricochet of plans gone awry.

Dragged, a jumping bean, I'm peeled
on a string tied to the back of banana seat.
Life stays two paces ahead of me,
and I followed close on its diamond heels,
a zero-sum game
with wins and losses all the same.

It took two fools to end a courtship,
a barrister and a softer pair of lips.
From each window of the M1 train northbound,
life's pageantry of dreams from the incubus
pass by, stop by stop,
wondering, "Which one's mine?
Where do I get off?"

When does this sentence end?
When does life stop taking tiny sips?
When can I guzzle the sky again?

Social Media and Literary Dalliance

Words,
those damned words,
they pour through me like
grains of sand
from the womb of the writer's mind
to the reader's heart.
And the hourglass is turned again.

Another hour passes
with the twist of a hand,
wee hours spent in the safe place
of our own unconsciousness.
But then I read and you write
to a stranger at night
and linger somewhere
along the spectrum of danger,
fanning from voyeur to vicarious empath.

I'm no deviant,
but there is something safe,
serenely satisfying,
in creative written exchanges
of anonymity between these sages,
whom we learn to hold so deeply
that people are how we imagine them to be
and we find anything beyond that futility.
It's absurd to share a soliloquy,
but I just did.

I Woke with Memory

I woke with a memory
I shouldn't have gone to bed with,
kicked in the stomach as I dreamt,
running from rejection.

Pages turned and burned, but not forgotten.
You didn't un-choose me.
You just succumbed to the ability
to love whomever your choice might be.

Lost in love with your options,
not with the man with whom you lie,
nor his spiritual vastness,
you love a love that dies.

'Tis destiny to play the jaded lover,
to paint a portrait with a precipitous cliff
so we can dream of open wings,
run toward the edge, and jump from it.

Join me out on the fringe of time.
Let's leap, dear lover.
Your fate is mine.
I'll grow wings, but yours will fail.
And you'll drop into darkness
through our thinning veil.

#Hashtag Poetry

#love takes a
#life, but be not
#sad for
#pain gives
#depression respite, but more that
#death gives life
#poetry so that in times of trouble it's
#you I see as a
#heart in a lighthouse for a
#poem lost at sea

***

"HelloPoetry" is an online poet's forum. Each day it publishes a list of the most popularly used hashtags from the submitted poems. I decided to take each word in the top-ten list and make it the first word of a ten-line poem. I called it "hashtag poetry." After I did this once, I realized that, every day, it's the same popular words in the same order. Each day always begins with #love.

What the Dead May Pray

Make us worthy in our dying,
for what we could not achieve in our living
for life subsumes death.
And while the evidence may show
we had not fully lived the way we'd hoped,
we are blessed with hope
that what failed to thrive
has died and departed the memory of others,
leaving us nothing but a clean slate
in the continued journey beyond life.

May all whom we've served
and against whom we've transgressed
step aside and cheer us on,
for the race is never over.

About the Author

Skip Maselli lives in northern Virginia, but resides somewhere between earth and heaven. Raised in the rural areas of southern New Jersey, far from the turnpike, he left for more remote parts of the earth, ending up in the most amazing places, from Korea to Europe, from Australia and the Pacific Rim to Turkey and southwest Asia, and points in between. Skip has been writing and reciting his poetry, prose, quips, and vignettes since he was 11 years old. The genre of his writing delves into various ontological explorations of mysticism, divine and human love, spiritual awakening, and socio-cultural and interpersonal musings. Indeed, you might find Sufi undertones in his writing. His first book, "Twenty-Five Words towards the Truth (#25wtT)" was published in March 2016.

Skip received his bachelor's degree from Dickinson College with a focus in geology and philosophy, a combination that at the time made perfect sense. After receiving his master's in civil and environmental engineering from the University of Wisconsin Skip served in the military, which provided him yet another view of the world. As an offset to his current career in business development for a large corporation he remains an impassioned reader, thinker, and deep listener. Many of his views have been shaped as a competitive swimmer and triathlete and spiritual explorationist. He is still called "Daddy" by his highly creative and gifted daughter Camerin, fifteen, and her wisely inquisitive brother, Aidan, twelve who lost their mother three years ago. His work and play reflect a life of inward travels, long drives, short phrases, small disappointments, big lessons – all flavored by serendipity, loving partnerships, and God-sent children and friends.

***

Author's photo credit (back cover): Taken by the young daughter of beloved friend, Dr. Omid Safi, at Agzikarahan Caravanserai, Cappadocia, 2013

Printed in the United States
By Bookmasters